THE KING'S GRACE

THE KING
Broadcasting at Sandringham

" May I add very simply and sincerely that if I may be regarded as in some true sense the head of this great and widespread family, sharing its life and sustained by its affection, this will be a full reward for the long and sometimes anxious labours of my reign of well-nigh five-and-twenty years."

THE KING'S GRACE

1910-1935

BY

JOHN BUCHAN

LONDON
HODDER AND STOUGHTON LIMITED
1935

THE KING'S GRACE PRESENTATION EDITION

First printed   -   April, 1935
Second impression May, 1935

THE KING'S GRACE PEOPLE'S EDITION

First printed   -   April, 1935
Sixth impression May, 1935

*Made and Printed in Great Britain for Hodder & Stoughton Limited
by Wyman & Sons Ltd., London, Reading and Fakenham*

" The Englishman is taught to love the King as his friend, but to acknowledge no other master than the laws which himself has contributed to enact."

GOLDSMITH : *Citizen of the World.*

PREFACE

THIS book is not a biography of the King, the time for which has happily not yet come, but an attempt to provide a picture—and some slight interpretation —of his reign, with the Throne as the continuing thing through an epoch of unprecedented change.

I have incorporated a few passages from my *History of the Great War*, published in 1922.

J. B.

CONTENTS

ILLUSTRATIONS

PART I

ILLUSTRATIONS

PART II

ILLUSTRATIONS

PART III

PROLOGUE

FOR fifteen centuries there have been kings in Britain, and for more than three hundred years there has been a single kingship. It has changed in character since the old monarchs, who ruled by virtue of their ownership of lands or their prowess in battle, but it has succeeded always in adapting itself to the changing character of our people. Like many of the deeper truths of government, it cannot be readily defined. Parliament can alter the laws at will, but the seventeenth-century doctrine still holds—that there is a " law fundamental," which may not be tampered with as long as the nation remains what it is. So kingship, which during the ages has shed much of its old power, yet maintains its central function, and continues to be a primary instinct of our people. A great revolutionary like Cromwell might upset one form of it, but only to spend himself in the effort to find another. We have rebelled against kings, but never against kingship.

In the last two hundred years, while the Throne has lost in definable powers, it has gained in significance. There have been wise monarchs and some not so wise, but the inherent and accumulated majesty of the office has increased. It is not only higher than any other human estate, but of a different kind from any other, for it is the mystical, indivisible centre of national union. It is the point around which coheres the nation's sense of a continuing personality. In any deep stirring of heart the people turn from the mechanism of government, which is their own handiwork and their servant, to that ancient, abiding thing behind governments, which they feel to be the symbol of their past achievement and their future hope.

But the Throne has altered in other things besides constitutional practice. It has come closer to the lives and interests of the citizen. The King is to-day far more a people's king than when an Edward or a Henry returned in triumph from the French wars. The office has come into the light of common day without losing its traditional glamour. Its dignity has not declined, but affection has been joined to reverence. Since the Tudors the phrase has been the King's Majesty. To-day the older form of words is the more fitting, the King's Grace.

There is nothing quite like the status of our Crown in the modern world, and I cannot find any close parallel in history. In law it can do no wrong ; its Ministers alone are responsible and accountable. In a season of turmoil it remains a *punctum indifferens*, a calm at the heart of the storm. The King is of no class, being above classes ; he is as much akin to the worker in the mine and to the labourer in the field as to the highest nobility. He can have no party bias, for his only bias is towards the whole people. He cannot initiate policies, though he creates the atmosphere that makes policies feasible. What is done in his name in the ordinary business of government is the work of others, and to them goes the blame or the credit. Of his own accord he does not interfere, unless there is a turning of distracted partisans to him, as to the traditional bulwark of the nation. Pinnacled above all, he is yet closer to the national consciousness than even the most famous Minister. His duty is not to act but to *be*, to represent the ultimate sanctities of the land which endure behind passing fevers and bewilderments : like Time,

> " who in the twilight comes to mend
> All the fantastic day's caprice."

When in a high mood of exaltation or sorrow the nation becomes a conscious unity and turns to him, then and only then does he intervene.

But the pedestal on which the King is placed is also a watch-tower. Having the whole people in his care, and having no prejudice of class or dogma or party, he is concerned only with the greater things, the profounder movements of national destiny. So in this year of his Silver Jubilee I have tried to present the spectacle of his reign with the Throne as the abiding background—such a spectacle as might be viewed from a high tower ; and to attempt what interpretation of its significance is permitted to one who is himself a dweller in the confused lowlands.

PART I

CHAPTER I

THE PAGEANT OF SUCCESSION

A NEW reign opens with ceremonial, the pageant of death and of life. A king has gone ; the King lives. On May 6th 1910 King Edward VII died. His body at first lay in state in the Throne Room of Buckingham Palace, whence it was conveyed in solemn procession to Westminster Hall. There for three days it rested on a great bier, guarded day and night by his soldiers, while all classes of his people filed silently past. On Friday May 20th came the State Funeral, when the dead king was carried through the thronged London streets on his way to Windsor, and was laid to rest in the vaults of St. George's Chapel with the stately rites which attend a monarch's burial. The voice of Garter King-at-Arms announced that it had pleased Almighty God to call a great prince out of this transitory world unto His Mercy, and that his son King George now reigned in his stead.

To the spectators who watched the *cortège* pass along the Mall in the bright May weather, it seemed that all the splendour of all the earth had come to pay its tribute. It seemed, too, that monarchy was entrenched in the world beyond fear of attack or decay. Besides the new King of England, eight kings followed the coffin—the German Emperor, the King of the Belgians, the sovereigns of Norway,

Greece and Spain, of Bulgaria, Portugal and Denmark. The ex-President of the United States, Theodore Roosevelt, was there, on his way home from his African hunting-trip, and there were some thirty royal princes apart from our own. It was not given to such a spectator to see the shadow of doom which hung over the glittering throng, or to guess what havoc the next decade would make with their thrones. Still less could he know that some of these figures would in a few years be protagonists in a drama which concerned the very existence of Britain. For in the procession were the Emperor William of Germany, his future ally King Ferdinand of Bulgaria, his future army commander, Prince Rupprecht of Bavaria, and the man destined to be his last Chancellor, Prince Maximilian of Baden ; King Albert of Belgium, who was to read Europe a lesson in kingly duty ; and the Archduke Franz Ferdinand of Austria, whose death was the tocsin that summoned the nations to war.

King Edward had reigned only nine years, but he had been long familiar to his people and his influence had been spread over many decades. His mother had in the end become an institution and a tradition, but he was always a vivid personality. He was a man whose talents were so well proportioned that in the aggregate they gave him a singular justness of perception. The long reign of Queen Victoria had prevented him from assuming responsibility in the plenitude of his powers, but the difficult apprentice-ship had enabled him to acquire a wide experience of public affairs, for he was always an assiduous worker. It had enabled him, too, to cultivate those social gifts which he possessed in a high degree—the power of laying his mind alongside others of every rank and race, a sensitiveness to atmosphere, a quick sympathy, and a warm humanity. He had few prejudices, either personal or national, and therefore he could see into the heart of many diverse classes and nations.

As a constitutional monarch he was above reproach, for, though some of his Ministers were more sympathetic to him than others, he made no favourites ; he never interfered in policy, though in the Budget crisis before his death and in the quarrel between Lords and Commons he exercised his right to counsel moderation. During his mother's last years Court ceremonial had become slipshod, and he restored it to its old decorum, for he had an acute sense of the proper appurtenances of a throne. To his people he was at once royal and homely ; he was what they looked for in a sovereign ; they understood him, and felt that in turn they were understood. He had dignity, but he had also a deep human kindness ; he enjoyed life and desired that others should enjoy it ; above all he was wholly sincere. He was widely popular, for he made the Crown a democratic institution. He was his people, and, in Mr. Asquith's words, had no self apart from them.

To have acquired such a repute was in itself a great achievement. In the sphere of foreign policy he was credited with having brought about positive results, notably a *rapprochement* with France. Undoubtedly the personal liking which he inspired among the French people contributed greatly to the breakdown of old suspicions, but in foreign affairs his conduct was always scrupulously regular. He did not attempt himself to start alliances ; he only made them possible. His purpose was always conciliation and peace. His nephew, the German Emperor, was one of the few people in the world of whom he was not altogether tolerant, but he did not permit this private lack of sympathy to bias him against the German nation. The dream of encircling Germany, with which he was credited, never entered into his head. His last visit to Vienna, which in Berlin was believed to be an attempt to seduce Austria from the Triple Alliance, was in fact devoted to seeking Austria's help to bring about a friendlier feeling between Germany and Britain.

The new King was about to complete his forty-fifth year. Eighteen years earlier he had become heir-presumptive on the death of his elder brother, the Duke of Clarence, and two years later he had married Princess Victoria Mary of Teck. Before that he had had a distinguished professional career as a sailor, serving in a variety of craft in many seas, and attaining in 1891 the rank of Commander. He relinquished the Navy on his brother's death, and his duties thenceforth were those which fall to an eventual wearer of the Crown. With a happy family circle as a background, he interested himself in every aspect of the nation's life. In 1899 he visited Ireland, and in the first year of his father's reign he and his wife travelled in the *Ophir* to Melbourne, opened the first Parliament of the Australian Commonwealth, and visited New Zealand, South Africa and Canada on their return journey. To the public he was not yet a familiar figure, but wherever he went he attracted affection, for he radiated friendliness and courtesy.

His father's Ministers were in an anxious mood, for

the times were unquiet, and the position of the Throne might soon be delicate. His reception of them gave them confidence. Mr. Asquith was "deeply moved by his modesty and good sense." At his first Council, held on May 7th, Sir Edward Grey was touched by the profound sorrow with which he spoke of his bereavement, and "the modesty and also the earnest public spirit with which he addressed himself to the task before him."

During the following months the customary deputations and addresses were received from every variety of public body. The Coronation was fixed for June 22nd 1911, and in the month preceding it a ceremony took place which was in the nature of a dramatic prologue. On May 16th came the unveiling of the new Queen Victoria Memorial in front of Buckingham Palace. The German Emperor, her grandson, was present in the uniform of a British Field-Marshal, the last occasion in which he was to be seen by the British people. The King, in his address, spoke words which were not only a tribute to a great Queen but were also a testimony to his conception of kingship :

As time passes and the years unfold, events are revealed in their true character and proportion. We are sure that the tribute we pay to-day will not be disputed by posterity. Her life was devoted to the discharge of her solemn public duty. Her authority was exercised on all occasions with sincere respect for constitutional usage and tradition. No Sovereign in history reigned so long over so many millions of mankind ; no ruler saw so many wonderful changes come to pass, or witnessed such a vast expansion in the scale and power of human arrangements ; no reign in this kingdom ever gathered up more carefully the treasures of the past, or prepared more hopefully the path of the future. No woman was ever held in higher honour. No Queen was ever loved so well.

25

THE KING'S GRACE

The Coronation of King Edward had been the first seen in England for sixty-five years. The new King's had not this novelty, but, unlike his father's, it did not take place under the shadow of war. It was a year of peace and of abounding prosperity, the weather was gracious, and crowds gathered such as London had never known. A Coronation is a domestic event, to which foreign countries send delegates but not their rulers ; but the Empire sent its Premiers, and it was the occasion of an Imperial Conference. No part of the great ceremony lacked its historic romance and spiritual significance ; the splendid procession through the streets of the capital ; the entry by the west door of the Abbey ; the Recognition, when the King showed himself to his people ; the music of Henry Purcell, who had written anthems for the Coronation of James II ; the Oath and the Anointing ; the presentation of the Spurs and the Sword ; the investiture with the Royal Robe ; the delivery of the Orb, the Ring and the Sceptre ; the supreme moment when the Archbishop of Canterbury placed on the King's head the Crown of St. Edward ; the presentation of the Bible with the words : " Here is wisdom ; this is the royal Law ; these are the lively Oracles of God " ; the Enthronement ; the homage of the Princes of the Blood and the Peers of the Realm ; the Coronation of the Queen ; the solemn Communion with the Threefold Amen of Orlando Gibbons, written for Charles I in Scotland ; the thunder of the *Te Deum* ; the last procession, when the Sceptre was laid on the Altar. It was, in the King's words which I have quoted, a gathering up of the treasures of the past and a preparing of the path of the future.

CHAPTER II

AN UNEASY HERITAGE

I

NO epoch in the life of a nation is exactly outlined by a sovereign's reign. The Victorian
Era contained many different stages, and the so-called
Edwardian Age was not a self-contained period,
exactly definable. In so far as it represented the
breakdown of nineteenth century security it began
long before the Queen's death, while certain vital
changes in the position of affairs and in the temper
of the people did not show themselves till after King
Edward had been several years on the throne. What
may fairly be said is that various forces moved in
the reign to a crescendo, and that what had hitherto
been conjecture was revealed as fact.

The nineteenth century began as an era of hope,
and till near its close was in Britain an era of
confidence. After its fashion it was an age of faith.
There is a passage in Mr. Gladstone's diary, under
the date January 19th 1834, which startles the
reader. At the age of twenty-five he returned for a
week-end to Oxford—almost his first visit to the place
since he had gone down. He had just entered
Parliament, and was already marked out as a rising
man. On such a visit the ordinary young politician
might be expected to spend his hours in conviviality,

27

perhaps a little in sentimental recollection, in friendly talk, in the natural ruffling of a distinguished stranger. The diary reveals that Mr. Gladstone devoted his time to the reading of " Pickering on Adult Baptism." I have no doubt that the book was dull, I suspect that it may have been futile, but the very name of it moves me like a spell. I see it, preposterous and yet magnificent, the symbol of a lost security of soul which was long ago dropped by the wayside.

The simpler Victorian confessions were assailed by the sceptical influence of a fast-developing physical science, and the iconoclast was at first as passionate in his faith as the orthodox. But about the nineties a certain languor set in in all belief. Most of the famous creeds, orthodox and heterodox alike, were shaken in popular esteem. They had either lost their votaries, having become disconsidered commonplaces, or a newer dialectic was questioning the authority even of the novelties. The nineteenth century had carried a full load of dogma ; the twentieth was sceptical of its predecessor's gods, and had not yet found those of its own which could awake the same serious fervour. The prevalent mood was in all things opportunist, and the bold reconstructions of earlier thinkers were out of fashion. The Victorian scepticism, which had led to strong anti-orthodox faiths, was replaced by a failure of intellectual vitality, and a mood which could be at once sceptical and credulous. In religion, in politics, in social science there was everywhere a tendency to exalt emotion and to appeal to the heart rather than to the head. When creeds were thus in solution, and there were few boundaries left fixed, the way was opened to those vague and potent eruptions of the human spirit

which, like the inroads of the Barbarians on the
Roman Empire, make a sharp breach with the past,
and destroy what they could not have created.

This weakening of intellectual foundations was
accompanied by an apparent loosening of civilisation's cement, which is a reverence for law and order
and a general good-will. A more violent, a less
equable temper was growing up in the world. Mr.
Churchill, so far as Britain was concerned, dates it,
probably with truth, from the Jameson Raid in 1896.
Thereafter politics became more feverish and party
feeling more extreme. This was true of all nations,
which seemed to be possessed by new ambitions and
new fears. Elsewhere it might be explained by a
dawning sense of insecurity ; in Britain the temper
was due largely perhaps to a wounded pride. In the
Victorian hey-day she had been the leader of Europe,
with her liberal institutions an acknowledged model
for her neighbours. That glory had passed, but in
the nineties it was replaced by a new vision of Empire.
Her possessions, acquired at random, were suddenly
seen as the material of a world-wide polity, which
offered illimitable opportunities to her youth. Her
poets sang of it with an Elizabethan passion, no
statesman omitted it from his perorations, and Mr.
Chamberlain was recognised as its business manager.

The ill-contrived South African War was like a
douche of icy water on this national confidence, and
it left a sobered but somewhat ill-tempered people.
The party game grew embittered. Liberals complained of the tactics of the Khaki election of 1900 ;
the tariff reform controversy was conducted with
surprising heat ; Conservatives in turn made a
grievance of the dear food and Chinese slavery cries ;

and the Liberal Government entered upon power in 1906 with popular enthusiasm behind it, but with its opponents in a temper which did not promise an easy course. "We see," Mr. Churchill has written, "a succession of partisan actions continuing without intermission for nearly twenty years, each injury repeated with interest, each oscillation more violent, each risk more grave, until at last it seemed that the sabre itself must be invoked to cool the blood and the passions that were rife." In her politics Britain seemed to have lost that common measure of agreement between parties which had been one of the secrets of her strength. In home affairs, as in the world at large, the former conventions and decencies were slipping out of public affairs.

In one respect the new century was the child of the old. The great discoveries of physical science had borne fruit in a vast increase of wealth and its wider diffusion. There was everywhere on the globe a feverish hunt for riches and a craze for luxury. If one form of self-confidence had weakened, another had been enlarged—a belief in the omnipotence of the huge scientific and social machine which had been created. If men were shy in the face of dogmas, they were confident about certain facts, and that manly humility which theology calls the fear of God was not a common mood. The power of plutocracies was everywhere in the ascendant, and the aristocracies, even the most ancient and reputable, found their prestige dwindling. In Britain the great families were still in the governing class, and the great houses were still maintained, but they counted for less. The catholic tastes of King Edward had opened fashionable society to many who a generation before would have knocked in vain at its doors. Much of this change was for the good, since it broke down old foolish barriers and did much to kill a false gentility. But it had also its malign effects, for it meant that the chief asset of the rich, their wealth, came to set the standard of life, and it tended to coarsen and vulgarise the public temper.

The increasing parade of luxury involved the growing discontent of the poor. It was a prosperous time ; unemployment, judged by later canons, was a small thing ; the standard of living and the conditions of labour among the working classes had been vastly improved. But the spread of education had made the worker ask questions, and the spectacle of wealth, which new facilities of transport and the popular press thrust under his notice, sharpened his interrogatories. Antagonism towards those in possession and a new class-consciousness were growing up among the dispossessed. Social democracy aimed at a revolution and a new world, and, following the example of its opponents, its aims were largely material. It sought rather to master the world's wealth than to regenerate the world's spirit. This aim, combined with the large share which the people had won in the government of most lands, led to an intense nationalism in practice, whatever might be the theory. The workers of one country, controlling the administration of that country, were prepared to set up any barrier that would secure the wealth which they sought to share from being pilfered by strangers. The consequence was that, while men were little disposed to contend for ideals as these used to be understood, they were very willing to struggle for material good things. The old romantic

nationalism had decayed, and in its place had come
a new nationalism of the pocket. Europe was moving
towards materialism and the self-contained and
jealous state.

It was a world which was still in the main good-
humoured, being comfortable, and there was much
goodwill about and much philanthropic experiment.
But it was a world without a strong common faith
and purpose, fumbling with ill-understood novelties,
already half the servant of the intricate machine it
had devised. It was a world self-satisfied without
contentment, a world in which prosperity was no
index to happiness. Mankind was drifting into
jealous cliques, while every day its economic bonds
became more subtly interlinked. Yet few recognised the danger signals. Only here and there a disconsidered prophet foretold that such a situation
could not endure, and that sooner or later must
come the thunderstroke to rend the lordly pleasure-
house.

In such a difficult " climate of opinion " the new
reign began.

II

The Liberal Government in power was a remarkable assembly of varied talents. Its first head, Sir
Henry Campbell-Bannerman, was indeed a man of
ordinary gifts, but he had great parliamentary skill
and a profound knowledge of human nature. He
had in full measure one half of the statesman's equip-
ment, for if he was not always subtle enough to
deal with things, he was simple enough to deal with
men. His successor, Mr. Asquith, was the classic

type of British statesman—an accomplished scholar, a successful lawyer, who brought a highly trained mind to the task of government. Mr. Morley at the India Office, Mr. Haldane at the War Office, Sir Edward Grey at the Foreign Office were also types which might be paralleled from many eras of our political history. But two ministers broke the traditional uniformity. Mr. Churchill was then only thirty-six, the heir to a famous parliamentary name, one who had already made his mark in soldiering and letters, and who sat a little loose from ordinary party interests, since his active mind was more concerned with fundamental problems than with party *expertise*. The other, Mr. Lloyd George, the Chancellor of the Exchequer, was a dozen years older, but had not lost the daring of youth. He was in touch, as no other Minister was, with the new currents of feeling in the British democracy, and his imagination and his instinct for what must come to be were drawing the Government into paths a little shocking to decorous Liberals.

Many causes had contributed to the Liberal victory of 1906—satiety with a party which had fought a costly and not very glorious war ; fear of the new protectionist crusade and its effect on the cost of living ; dislike of the Chinese labour experiment in South Africa. But one potent reason was that historic Liberalism, repressed since 1895, now for the last time mustered its forces. Its devotees, chiefly older men who had known Mr. Gladstone's spell, held their creed with an almost religious fervour. Its articles were the maintenance of free trade, disestablishment, free and non-sectarian education, Irish Home Rule, temperance, peace, and a modest social

33

reform. To the advocacy of these large aims it brought a long tradition of expert electioneering. It was hostile especially to Mr. Balfour's Education Act of 1902, which permitted rate aid to denominational schools ; a somewhat narrow margin of dispute, which Mr. Balfour ironically described as an identification of " the frontier which eternally separates right and wrong with the transient line which technically distinguishes local from national taxation."

The new Government was not fortunate in meeting the wishes of its oldest and most loyal supporters. Chinese labour was indeed brought to an end, and this necessarily led Sir Henry Campbell-Bannerman to devise and carry through the greatest achievement of his career—the grant of self-government to the new South African colonies, which in 1909 was followed by an Act establishing the Union of South Africa. But the Education Bill to redress Mr. Balfour's wrongdoing was rejected by the Lords. A Plural Voting Bill was rejected by the Lords, a Licensing Bill was rejected, and other measures were cruelly emasculated. Only a Trade Disputes Bill, which restored peaceful picketing, safeguarded trade union funds, and took strikes out of the law of conspiracy, was permitted to pass by the Upper House on the not very defensible ground that it did not wish a quarrel with Labour. The Government with its huge majority was beginning to fall into discredit. Such a majority is apt to be a misfortune, for it is inclined to lead rather than to follow, and to keep it together means a strict attention to the prejudices of the often ignorant rank and file. It was necessary to win back respect by leaving the conventional rut —those ancient causes which woke enthusiasm only

34

among elderly loyalists. Mr. Lloyd George came forward as the Greatheart to lead his party to the Promised Land. The reforms which he proposed could be embodied in a Budget, on which no House of Lords would dare to lay sacrilegious hands.

So in the Budget of 1908 a scheme of Old Age Pensions was included, and was duly passed into law. But in 1909 Mr. Lloyd George unmasked his full batteries. For his proposed system of sickness and unemployment insurance he needed money, and in his Budget of that year he proposed to raise the extra fourteen millions partly by an increase of the income tax, super-tax and death duties, and partly by taxes on undeveloped land and on land's unearned increment. The Conservative party were stirred to fury. They did not confine themselves to criticism of the dubious land taxes, but denounced the whole programme as a policy of spoliation and a class vendetta ; its only logical justification, they said, was the anarchist maxim that all property was theft ; it was a wicked attempt to rouse a class war. Mr. Lloyd George did not conciliate his opponents by his methods of defence, which were mainly picturesque vituperation of the " haves " on behalf of the " have nots." The serious argument for his policy—that the time had come when the State must concern itself more closely with the life of the citizen, and that the citizen must pay for it—a doctrine to which most thinking men consented—was scarcely heard in the hubbub ; if it had been, it would have deeply disquieted many orthodox Liberals.

The House of Lords, after a good deal of heartsearching, rejected the Budget by a large majority, on the ground that it was not a measure to raise the

necessary revenues for the year, but an attempt to
work a revolution through a finance bill. The
reason alleged by the Lords was intelligent enough,
whatever may be thought of their tactical wisdom.
Matters had now come to the point of crisis. The
Upper House, so far from being an independent
Second Chamber, was, it appeared, only an appanage
of the Conservative party, which with its aid was
always in power, whoever might be in office. It had
already massacred a host of Liberal innocents, and
now the cup of its iniquities was full. It had challenged the central and historic privilege of the House
of Commons. An appeal to the country was necessary, and the Prime Minister made it clear that he
asked from the electorate not only an approval of
the Budget but a mandate to bring the Lords to
reason. He carried a resolution in the House of
Commons that their action was " a breach of the
Constitution and a usurpation of the rights of the
Commons," and in a speech at the Albert Hall he
announced : " We shall not hold office until we
can secure the safeguards which experience shows us
to be necessary to the legislative utility and the
honour of the party of progress. . . . We are going
to ask the electors to say that the House of Lords
shall be confined to the proper objects of a second
chamber. The absolute veto must go." He was
reverting to the scheme of a suspensory veto which
John Bright had once fathered, and which in 1907
had been the subject of a resolution proposed by Sir
Henry Campbell-Bannerman.

The election of January 1910 had an unexpected
result. The Government majority, which in 1906
had been 356, was now only 124. Moreover, 82 of it

were Irish, and, if the Irish voted with the Opposition, the Government would fall. Now the Irish had not loved the Budget, and, indeed, had opposed it on the second reading. In Great Britain the election had been fought chiefly on that Budget, no constituency showing much interest in the Lords question. The result was a mandate for Mr. Lloyd George's policy, but only if the Irish supported it, and for that they must have their reward in the shape of a Home Rule Bill. No Home Rule Bill, however, would pass the Lords in their present form ; therefore as a necessary preliminary the Second Chamber must be dealt with. For a week or two the fate of the Government hung in the balance. The Cabinet was by no means united, the Prime Minister desiring to confine himself to the suspensory veto, while other ministers were anxious to link this with Second Chamber reform. The Opposition had been presented with a formidable cry. The Lords were to be attacked not for their faults but for their virtues ; they were the only barrier against secession, and their destruction was the price to be paid for the precious Budget to separatists who were otherwise hostile to Mr. Lloyd George's adventure.

The danger was tided over. In early April the House of Commons carried three resolutions on the subject of the Lords and the first reading of the Parliament Bill which embodied them. The Irish having been thus appeased, the Budget passed through both Houses on April 20th, the Lords reserving their fire. The King's death found Government and Opposition ordering their battle lines for a constitutional clash of the first magnitude.

Side by side with these heavy domestic preoccupations, Ministers from 1906 onward had to carry a burden of external cares—grave problems of foreign policy and defence. These for the most part had to be kept secret ; they could not be shared with their followers or give opportunity for moving perorations.

Ever since the close of the South African War a certain satiety with overseas politics had fallen upon the British people. The dream of imperialism, the closer union of the British race in one great pacific commonwealth, had lost something of its glamour, tending to sink to a form of race chauvinism or a mere scheme of commercial protection. Imperialism had at its best meant a political vision extending beyond these shores, and, as it faded in popular esteem, the British people inclined more and more to be absorbed in internal problems. There had been a time in their history when, under Palmerston and Gladstone and Disraeli, foreign affairs had been an integral part of their interests, and elections had been lost and won on diplomatic programmes. But for twenty years the doings of Europe had concerned them little. The imperialist who thought that Britain was an extra-European Power depending on the control of the sea, and the social reformer who regarded foreign policy as a lure to distract the nation from more urgent matters, had alike contributed to this result.

In 1910 the people of Britain were less alive to the significance of what might happen beyond their borders than many a humble continental state. To an electorate excited by partisan warfare, dragooned by sleepless party caucuses, and scared or exhilarated by the prospect of large social changes, the husks of foreign policy were not acceptable. Warnings of the possibility of war were regarded as merely a trick to distract. Expenditure on defence was a waste of money which might be spent on objects from which there was a sound return. These things had no electioneering value, and the comfortable delusion was fostered that, so long as Britain chose to desire peace, peace would follow. There were men in the Government who to their honour refused to prophesy smooth things, but the cotton-wool with which the atmosphere was thick deadened their warnings.

Yet in a sense this public apathy was a fortunate thing, for it enabled weighty matters to be discussed, as it were, *in camera*. When King Edward ascended the throne Britain stood in a perilous isolation. She was disliked by Germany, suspected by France, and looked upon by Russia as the eternal enemy. When he died she had been brought again into the European family. By an alliance with Japan she had safeguarded her position in the Far East. There was an understanding with France, daily becoming more cordial, and one of the first acts of the new Liberal Government had been to authorise conversations between the British and the French army staffs with a view to collaboration should the need arise. The defeat of Russia by Japan had turned the mind of the former away from more distant parts of a globe where her interests might have clashed with ours, certain outstanding questions with Britain

39

had been settled, and her alliance with France made her more complaisant towards a country which was France's friend. Britain was now to all intents an associate of the Dual Alliance, though the fact was scarcely realised by the majority of her people. The Triple Entente had come into being.

We had entered the European game at a disturbed moment. The cat-fish in the pool was Germany. If she had discarded Bismarck's policy, as well as the subtlety of his methods, the arrogant spirit of the Iron Chancellor remained. She felt, not without reason, that her dignity had been offended by the agreement between Britain and France which settled the questions of Morocco and Egypt without consulting her, and in the spring of 1905 Prince Bülow suggested to his master that the occasion had come for a dramatic *coup* to retrieve his country's weakened prestige. On the last day of March in that year the Emperor landed with a retinue at Tangier, proclaimed the integrity of Morocco, promised the Sultan to defend his independence, and demanded that the whole Moroccan question should be reopened. A weak cabinet in Paris bent to the storm, M. Delcassé, the Foreign Minister, was sacrificed, and a conference of the Powers was summoned at Germany's instigation. But for her the result was a bitter disappointment. She was revealed as, except for her faithful Austria, alone in the world ; Italy deserted her colleagues of the Triple Alliance and supported her Latin neighbour ; Britain and Russia stood solidly beside France. The Algeciras arrangement of April, 1906, provided no lasting settlement, but it made clear the new grouping of the European peoples. Germany had irritated and alarmed the world by showing too nakedly her hand. It was certain that she would look forthwith for fresh methods to satisfy her pride.

Her next *coup* was more adroitly handled. In the summer of 1908 the old regime in Turkey was swept away by revolution, the Young Turk party came into power, and by their liberal professions attracted for a little the sympathy of Western Europe. At first the change seemed against Germany's interests, for she had sedulously cultivated the Hamidian Government, and would have to start again from the beginning. But she saw a chance of fishing profitably in the troubled waters. Austria seized the occasion to annex the Turkish provinces of Bosnia and Herzegovina, of which she had long had the administration. Serbia was alarmed, for she saw her hope of union with the Bosnian Serbs extinguished. Russia, as Serbia's protector, shared her annoyance at this annulment of the work of the Congress of Berlin, and Italy was disquieted by Austria's advance into the Balkan peninsula. But Austria had Germany at her back, and the protests of the Triple Entente were received with a cool contempt. The Emperor William made his famous speech about Germany's "shining armour," and the Entente, unprepared for a European War in such a cause, had to acquiesce with the best grace it could muster. It was a proof of the strong foundations of the new friendship between France, Britain and Russia that it survived unimpaired so grievous a diplomatic defeat. The situation had been anxious, and Mr. Asquith told Mr. Balfour that he had never known Europe nearer to war.

The first German move had failed at Algeciras ; the second had succeeded ; the third was to end in a dangerous fiasco. It came in the spring of 1911.

There had been a revolt in Fez and French troops had entered the city. To Germany it seemed that the Shereefian Empire was breaking up, and she was determined to share in the spoils. If France was to have the task of reconstructing the country, Germany must have territorial compensation ; in the words of her Foreign Minister, " If one wants to eat peaches in January, one must pay for them." The gunboat *Panther* was despatched to Agadir, and the German press claimed Western Morocco as their country's right. But France in 1911 was not the France of 1905. M. Caillaux, who showed signs of temporising with Germany, was swept from power, and the new Ministry, under Raymond Poincaré, included Delcassé, who was not inclined to truckle to Berlin. Britain sent a warship to Agadir to lie alongside the *Panther*, and proclaimed in unmistakable terms her support of France. Germany, not yet ready for a world-war, abated her pretensions, and the Moroccan question was settled by various cessions of territory by France in Central Africa.

All through that summer, during the ceremonies of the Coronation and the bitter dispute about the Lords, Ministers had on their hands this controversy which presently might reach flash-point. There was a day in August when the crash seemed likely to come before the week was out. The affair had two important consequences. Hitherto it had been supposed, especially in Germany, that the Cabinet was not united in this matter, and undoubtedly a large section of the Liberal party was averse to any foreign commitments and suspicious of any increase in the national defences. But now the idol of this group, Mr. Lloyd George himself, announced to the world that a pacific Britain did not stand for peace at any price. In a speech at the Mansion House on July 21st he declared that " if a situation were to be forced upon us in which peace could only be preserved by the surrender of the great and beneficent position which Britain has won by centuries of heroism and achievement, by allowing Britain to be threatened where her interests are vitally affected, as if she were of no account in the Cabinet of Nations, then I say emphatically that peace at that price would be a humiliation intolerable for a great country like ours to endure." These words revealed to an audience, which comprised his foremost critics, another side of the man ; he was " varminty," as an admiring sportsman put it, in other things than class warfare. The second consequence was that Germany was filled with a sullen fury against France, and not less against Britain, her ally. From that moment her war party dropped all talk of compromise and pursued naked aggression.

The burden of this foreign crisis, the duty of watching every move and of persuading an unwilling nation to prepare adequate defences, fell, apart from the Prime Minister, especially upon two men, Sir Edward Grey and Mr. Haldane, to whom was now added Mr. Churchill, the new First Lord of the Admiralty. Mr. Haldane, an enthusiast for German philosophy and letters, had, with the consent of King Edward, paid a visit to Berlin in the summer of 1906 to examine the possibility of a friendly under-standing, and had reached the conclusion that, while there were dangerous forces at work within the German polity, the influence of the Emperor and his chief advisers was on the side of peace. To cherish this inclination and to nurse it into a steady warmth must be the object of Britain, and meantime at the War Office he laboured to make the British army a fit instrument for the task which might one day fall to it.

Sir Edward Grey worked to the same end. Representing a very ancient and honourable type in British statecraft, the country gentleman with no vulgar ambitions who would have much preferred a private station, he had toiled in office to maintain the peace of Europe, and his grave simplicity of character, his moral dignity, and his gift of sound judgment and conciliatory statement had done much to keep the tottering fabric together. But no man was more conscious than he that he was treading a hazardous road. He was accustoming Britain to interfere in continental affairs when she was not armed on a continental scale, and when the whole trend of her immediate interests was away from national defence. If Germany chose to be arrogant he could not compel humility, for he had no adequate sanction behind him. To an ally he could not promise such immediate assistance as would enable her to speak with her foe in the gate. His arms were historical prestige, wealth, a great navy ; but these were not quite *in pari materia* with those of the Powers with whom he thought to treat. He was a voice, a grave, reasonable, weighty voice, but behind it was not the appropriate weapon.

Ministers during the summer of 1911 might well have had wrung from them Lord Salisbury's cry that " politics was a cursed profession." They had on their hands a domestic programme which had evoked wild excesses of partisanship, and had attracted to them an odium from at least one-half of the people

44

which had been unknown since the first Reform Bill.
They were committed to a policy of constitutional
change of which they could not foresee the end.
And behind it all they saw a fermenting Europe,
which promised perilous brews and deadly gasses, a
Europe of which the larger part of their following
was wholly ignorant—and must be kept ignorant,
since a popular scare would beyond doubt kill all
chance of a peaceful settlement. Mr. Churchill has
well described the comfortless dualism of their lives.

Those whose duty it was to watch over the safety of the
country lived simultaneously in two different worlds of thought.
There was the actual visible world with its peaceful activities
and its aims ; and there was a hypothetical world, a world
" beneath the threshold," as it were, a world at one moment
utterly fantastic, at the next seeming about to leap into reality
—a world of monstrous shadows moving in convulsive combina-
tions through vistas of fathomless catastrophe.

IV

In such an hour of strife and confusion at home
and of crisis abroad the new King was called upon
to make a grave decision.

The powers of a constitutional monarch must
always be indeterminate and delicate, brittle if too
heavily pressed, a shadow if tactlessly advertised,
substantial only when exercised discreetly in the
background. But they are none the less real for that,
since he has the privilege and duty of advising his
advisers (the phrase was Sir Wilfrid Laurier's), the
custody of his custodians ; and he may have in the
last resort the heavier duty of deciding on his own
account a weighty constitutional problem. The
prerogative may have to be called in to cut the tangle.

The first task King Edward had skilfully and happily performed. He rather liked a political crisis, and Lord Esher has told us that he enjoyed the excitement caused by Mr. Chamberlain's resignation in 1903. He had protested to the Prime Minister about the platform style of his Chancellor of the Exchequer, protests which Mr. Lloyd George received with complete good humour and with unfulfilled promises of amendment. He had endeavoured to avert the rejection of the Budget by the House of Lords, and had summoned Lord Lansdowne and Mr. Balfour to confer with him. The second duty he was not yet called upon to face, but he saw it approaching. He saw that the problem of the Second Chamber had been raised and could not be dropped, and the resolutions passed by the Commons in December, 1909, and Mr. Asquith's pre-election speeches made the Government policy clear. He did not like it ; he thought it meant the destruction of the House of Lords ; he had his own scheme of reform, which he discussed with Lord Crewe at Windsor in January, 1910, and which would have confined the right of voting to one hundred peers.

After the election King Edward realised that the crisis was near. A bill would be introduced to limit the power of the Lords ; they would not accept it : what then ? A dissolution would not help matters if the nation returned the same verdict. If government was to be carried on, the only way was the use of the royal prerogative. A request to know the Cabinet's intention brought, on February 11th, the discreet reply that Ministers did not propose to advise any exercise of the prerogative until the actual necessity arose. Ten days later Mr. Asquith announced that he had sought no guarantee from the King and had received none ; it would be wholly improper to ask in advance for a blank authority. But private conversations had carried the matter further. The King had made it clear that he recognised that the new Parliament Bill must go on the statute-book if the nation plainly demanded it, but he asked that the nation's approval should be sought by an election fought definitely upon that issue. The Prime Minister was therefore justified in assuming that, if this condition was carried out and the result of the election was a decisive verdict, the royal prerogative would be brought into play to give that verdict effect. " In no case," he told the House of Commons on April 14th, " will we recommend dissolution except under such conditions as will secure that in the new Parliament the judgment of the people as expressed in the election will be carried into law."

King Edward's death in May flung everything into the melting-pot. Could not some way be found of settling the quarrel which would not force upon a new and inexperienced monarch the necessity of a difficult decision ? Moreover, the King's death had revived a feeling for our historic institutions which took some of the heart out of the Liberal crusade. A conference was agreed upon, and eight honest gentlemen, four from each side, sat down in June round a table to try to settle terms. At first they seemed to be making progress, but very soon it appeared that neither side had sufficient small change with which to purchase the assent of the other. There were not enough free assets to bargain with. The Conservative members desired that measures involving constitutional change should be put into a separate category, but under " constitutional " there fell the business of Irish Home Rule, on which the fate of the Government depended. Few people were surprised, and many were relieved, when on November 11th it was announced that the Conference had drawn to a fruitless close.

The time had come to approach the new King to discover if he took his father's view. On November 11th the Prime Minister went to Sandringham and put the matter fully before him. The King had hoped for much from the Conference, and was greatly distressed at its failure, but he realised that the responsibility must now lie on his own shoulders. If a deadlock came, the opposition of the Lords could be overcome only by limiting or increasing their numbers. The first way—of withholding writs of summons—was invidious and possibly unconstitutional, but the prerogative of new creation was undoubted and had fairly recent parallels. In Mr. Asquith's view the mere knowledge that such a step was contemplated would probably bring about agreement. On the 15th the Cabinet drew up and dispatched to Sandringham a memorandum which advised an immediate dissolution. " His Majesty's Ministers cannot take the responsibility of advising a dissolution, unless they understand that in the event of the policy of the Government being approved by an adequate majority in the new House of Commons, His Majesty will be ready to exercise his constitutional powers, which may involve the prerogative of creating Peers, if needed, to secure that effect shall be given to the decision of the country." Next day Mr. Asquith and Lord Crewe went to Buckingham Palace for their answer.

The King liked the Lords policy of the Government no more than his father had done. To him it seemed the destruction of an ancient and precious thing. Burdened as he was with the thought of the foreign situation, he felt that it would not increase our prestige in the world " to see Britannia," as Lord Rosebery put it, " in her old age casting away her helmet . . . apparently prepared to revise at ten days' notice the constitution of eight hundred years." But what other course remained ? If the coming election showed a clear popular verdict, the obstinacy of the Lords would mean the Cabinet's resignation. A Conservative Government would not survive for a week, and in the dissolution which must follow the Sovereign would become a subject of debate, and that kingship of which he was the trustee would be grievously compromised. After a long discussion he said that he saw no other way but to assent to the Cabinet's advice. He made one proviso—that the Parliament Bill should be submitted to the House of Lords before the election. Mr. Asquith had not received a guarantee in the formal sense, but he had achieved what he described as a " hypothetical understanding."

The December election removed the hypothetical element, for the Government was returned with a majority of one hundred and twenty-six. In January the King insisted on having an interview with Lord Lansdowne at Windsor, not to ask for advice but to find out at first-hand the views of the Opposition—a perfectly correct step, to which surprisingly Mr. Asquith at first raised objections. But the air was electric and even the stout nerve of the Prime Minister was shaken. The Parliament Bill was introduced in

49

the Commons on February 22nd, and early in May
had been carried through all its stages. The Lords
had sought at first to counter it with their own
scheme of reform, but the atmosphere was not
congenial to the construction of a brand-new Second
Chamber, one of the most difficult enterprises of
statecraft. The Coronation interrupted the debates
for the better part of a month, and they were resumed
by the Lords in a rising temper. Amendments were
carried there which wholly altered the measure, and
on July 14th the Cabinet submitted a memorandum
to the King, pointing out that the expected deadlock
was approaching, in which " it will be the duty
of Ministers to advise the Crown to exercise its
prerogative."

Up till then no mention had been made by
Mr. Asquith or his colleagues of the understanding
arrived at in the previous November. But now it
was necessary to make it plain to the Conservative
leaders, in the hope that the knowledge might enable
them to control their followers. The King himself
was anxious that the facts should be published. So
on July 20th Mr. Asquith wrote to Lord Lansdowne
and Mr. Balfour to inform them that the House of
Commons could not accept the Lords amendments ;
that, should the need arise, the Government would
advise the King to exercise his prerogative by the
creation of new peers ; and that His Majesty had
been pleased to signify that he would act on this
advice. It was the signal for violent outbursts. On
July 24th the Prime Minister was shouted down in
the Commons. Votes of censure were moved in
both Houses, and Ministers were accused of having
shattered constitutional etiquette in the interest of

a corrupt bargain over Irish Home Rule. On
August 8th Lord Crewe, in the Lords, explained
what had happened at the interview with the King
the previous November, and how there had been no
request for unconditional guarantees.

The final debate there on August 10th and 11th
was tense and dramatic. Lord Lansdowne urged
that the Bill be passed lest a worst thing should befall,
but the irreconcilables under Lord Halsbury refused
to yield. Lord Morley, who had at first been opposed
to the use of the prerogative, read a formula which
the King had approved : " If the Bill should be
defeated to-night His Majesty will consent to the
creation of peers sufficient in number to guard
against any possible combination of the different
parties in opposition by which the Parliament Bill
might be exposed a second time to defeat." Till the
last moment no one dared to forecast the result. In
the end the majority of the peers abstained, and the
measure became law by one hundred and thirty-one
votes to one hundred and fourteen, thirty-seven
Conservatives and thirteen bishops voting with the
Government.

It was a controversy which interested the politicians
rather than the people of Britain. The ordinary
man would probably have resented the abolition of
the House of Lords, but he had no objection to it
being taught its place. Under the Parliament Act
it was deprived of all control over the Budget of the
year, if certified as a money Bill by the Speaker, and
its power of rejection was limited to measures sent
up no oftener than twice within two years by the
Commons. To those who argued that the whole

scheme was slovenly and unscientific there was no real answer, except that this was the way that changes had always come to Britain. Elaborate constitutional reform in cold blood seems to be beyond our national capacity ; we correct an immediate abuse by a piece of hasty extemporisation, and trust to Providence to make it work. We have always preferred the provisional to the absolute. The Parliament Act turned part of our constitution into a written word, but it did not finish the sentence ; there was no full-stop, only a line of dashes.

But to the King, just entering upon his reign, the situation was most delicate and perplexing. He had not behind him his father's wide political experience. He had had no training in the *arcana imperii*, the imponderables of our paradoxical government. He was dependent upon the counsel of one set of advisers ; etiquette forbade him to take advice from their opponents ; his personal suite might be consulted, but they were not experts ; in the end he had to act alone. In these difficult circumstances he behaved with strict constitutional probity, because he had to guide him that instinct which he shared with the majority of his subjects—the good sense of the plain man. In this common touch was to lie the true secret of his power. The Parliament Bill wrangle was an auspicious beginning.

CHAPTER III

THE RESTLESS YEARS

I

IN November 1911 the King and Queen sailed for India. In his proclamation of November 2nd 1908, on the fiftieth anniversary of the assumption of the Government of India by the Crown, King Edward had declared that he looked back " on the labour of the past half-century with clear gaze and good conscience." The words were justified, for history records no wiser and more generous example of imperial rule. The charter of modern India was the royal proclamation of 1858, in which Queen Victoria guaranteed existing rights, and offered to the Indian people the hope of a partnership in government. " We desire no extension of our present territorial possessions ; and while we will permit no aggression upon our dominions or our rights to be attempted with impunity, we shall sanction no encroachment on those of others. We shall respect the rights, dignity and honour of native princes as our own. . . . It is further our will that, so far as may be, our subjects of whatever class or creed be fully and freely admitted to any offices the duties of which they may be qualified by their education, abilities and integrity duly to discharge." These sentences were a pledge the purpose of which was clear, but the interpretation of which might not be easy.

A succession of Viceroys had toiled at the interpretation. The Viceregal ritual, stiff as cloth-of-gold, was well calculated to maintain the majesty of the Throne, but behind its magnificence lay a most arduous and practical toil. In administration, in economics, in education there had been steady progress in the direction of drawing the people of India into a closer partnership in government and in fitting them for that partnership. But the work was yearly becoming more difficult. The wider diffusion of Western education was bringing in Western ideas which, transplanted to an alien soil, often assumed fantastic forms. Britain's laggard victory in the South African War had lowered her prestige ; above all, the rise of Japan, and her triumph over Russia, had inflamed the pride of all Eastern peoples and dulled the glamour which had once attended the white races. Lord Curzon's viceroyalty, too, a monument of courage, industry and far-sighted devotion, had perhaps provided for India a diet which, for all its high quality, was too large in quantity for ready digestion.

India was uneasy, and when Lord Minto went there in 1905 he found a stirring on the face of the waters. Crimes of violence were increasing, ugly secret movements were afoot, and even honest men were beginning to chafe under paternal government, and to demand that they should be permitted to blunder for themselves. It was necessary to adopt coercive measures, but Lord Minto and Mr. Morley, the Secretary of State, were convinced that reform should go hand in hand with a firm rule. Accordingly

the Indian Councils Act in 1909 made a modest
start in representative government. Lord Minto considered that much of the unrest was perfectly loyal,
and neither he nor Mr. Morley had any intention
of what the latter called " loosening the bolts " of
British power and responsibility. Their view of
India was that of Mill—" a kingly government, free
from the control, though strengthened by the support,
of representative institutions." But it was clear that
they had taken the first step on a path whose direction
could not be foreseen, and that their structure was
at the best provisional, since an immovable executive
and an irresponsible legislature could not, according
to the lessons of history, make for harmony.

In such an atmosphere of uncertainty and disquiet the royal visit took place. Its purpose was wise,
for the Throne was the basis of our Indian rule—that
part of our complex government which the humblest
Indian peasant understood and reverenced. Moreover, the oriental mind appreciates the outward
trappings and the visible emblems of royalty, and is
impressed and inspired by ceremonial. Already in
the winter of 1905 their Majesties, as Prince and
Princess of Wales, had visited the country and had
been received with enthusiasm. Now the visit was
a matter of high state. The King had come in
person to announce his coronation, and, as is the
secular custom of the East on such occasions, to
commemorate it by certain marks of especial favour.

The journey was one long triumphal procession
and, whatever were the hidden fires, no smoke from
them marred the splendid ceremonies. The King's
speeches were extraordinarily happy. At Bombay he
reminded his hearers that the city had once been

55

the dowry of a British queen. On the historic Ridge of Delhi he addressed the Imperial Legislative Council, and to municipalities and universities he spoke of India's problems with sympathy and knowledge. The supreme occasion was the great Coronation Durbar at Delhi. On December 7th their Majesties made a state entry into the ancient Mogul capital. A vast new city of camps had sprung up almost in a night, a hint to the discerning of what the principal " boon " was to be. On the 12th, in a scene in which the long-descended pageantries of both East and West were mingled, the King spoke from the throne to the Indian princes and people, and received the homage of feudatories and subjects. " I rejoice," he said, " to have this opportunity of renewing in my own person those assurances which have been given you by my revered predecessors of the maintenance of your rights and privileges, and of my earnest concern for your welfare, peace and contentment."

Then he announced the boons. As a concession to native feeling the partition of Bengal would be reversed, and that presidency constituted a Governorship, with a new Lieutenant-Governorship in Council for Behar, Chota Nagpur and Orissa, and a Chief Commissionership for Assam. But the principal change was that the Government of India would be transferred from Calcutta to the traditional capital, Delhi, and that a new imperial city would arise there. Three days later he laid its foundation stones.

The announcement was received with excitement, surprise, commendation, but also with criticism which has not yet died away. It was beyond question a bold step, inspired by that rare thing in policy, imagination. It linked the record of the British Raj with another famous page in India's history. It was grateful to the Mohammedan section of the people. The new seat was in the heart of India, and not in the eastern corner, and so had certain political and strategic advantages. But it was a slight to Bengal, though she had received compensation, and it involved a vast expenditure by a not over-rich land. The most serious criticism was that made at home by ex-Viceroys like Lord Curzon and Lord Minto, that its direct association with the King-Emperor's visit put upon the Sovereign the responsibility for a scheme which at the best involved what Burke called " great varieties of untried being." Its true justification was as a symbolic act. If India was about to enter upon a new course it was well that there should be a dramatic departure from the tradition of John Company and a return to what had been the glory of an earlier Empire.

II

The King came back in February to a greyer but not more peaceful scene. I have called the years 1912 and 1913 the restless years, and in the retrospect they seem a period of continuous effervescence and ferment. Even at the time one was conscious of walking on unsubstantial ground. Behind all the self-confidence of prosperity there was a sense of impermanence, as if good things would not last, and black clouds were banking beyond the horizon. At home there was constant agitation, but not, as in the past, as part of a coherent and rational plan. Most of the clamour was apt to be episodic and unrelated, demanding specific things without troubling about what in the long run the effect might be. It seemed to be rather evidence of short tempers and jangled nerves than of serious purpose.

The difficulties with Labour were a case in point. The Government had done much to put the trade unions in a privileged position, and had overridden certain ancient common law principles for the purpose. On the day that the Lords passed the Parliament Bill the House of Commons decided upon the payment of members, a step admittedly taken in the interest of Labour. But Labour was not content, and presently the Government found itself compelled to depart from the old custom of letting the parties in an industrial dispute fight it out between themselves. People had been slow to realise the change in the temper of British Labour which had been coming in the previous decade. The cheap press had informed the working man of many things about which he had once been ignorant. He understood as never before the huge profits which capital was earning, and naturally desired a larger share. The Liberal victory in 1906 had excited his hopes. The bold experiments in social reform of the new Government had whetted his appetite. He had come to realise not only his needs and his rights, but his strength in combination. In every great industry there was a grumbling discontent—in the railways, in the cotton mills, among seamen and dockers and transport workers, above all in the coal mines. Strikes broke out like jets of steam from volcanic soil, and, however trivial the professed cause, they showed an ugly tendency to extend both their area

58

and their purpose. The sympathetic strike was becoming more than an example of human *camaraderie* ; it was proof now of the solidarity in purpose and spirit of great masses of men.

In the hot summer of 1911, at the height of the Agadir crisis, there had been a railway strike after twenty-four hours notice, a strike of both skilled and unskilled employees, for the Amalgamated Society and the Engineers and Firemen were acting along with the General Railway Workers. A strike was now a matter not of minor tactics but of grand strategy. This one was soon settled by the promise of a special commission of inquiry. But in March 1912 came something more serious, a miners' strike for a national minimum wage, which, beginning in Wales, brought out more than a million men in the different coalfields. This was a new and disquieting thing, a nation-wide strike in a key industry, which if it continued might dislocate the whole of the country's life. The Government, which might have been content to keep the ring in a local or sectional dispute, was compelled to interfere. Within a week it passed through both Houses a Bill which admitted the principle of a minimum wage and provided local machinery for fixing it, and the miners, not without difficulty, were brought back to work by the middle of April, having secured the larger part of their demands. Mr. Asquith, called to a novel task, had met it in a way which, he was satisfied, did not conflict with the Liberal creed. To fix a wage by act of Parliament would be an impossible paternalism, but it was another thing to provide the apparatus for fixing it by local and expert knowledge.

Yet no ingenuity could disguise the boldness of the

59

innovation, and no optimism could blind thinking men to the dangerous pass to which the industrial world was hastening. Trade unions were becoming a power which might soon dictate harshly to the nation. There was theory behind it, the dogmas of syndicalism and Marxian socialism, and sober Englishmen were beginning to talk a strange jargon, but to the ordinary trade unionist doctrine had little to do with it. The plain fact was that he was becoming conscious of his strength, and resolute to use that strength to maintain what he considered to be his rights. He was beginning to see possibilities in direct action, for, if that caused not only loss of wealth to certain employers but a paralysis of the national life, then he could talk with any Government in the gate.

If Labour was becoming self-conscious, so was Capital. Alarmed by the Government's social experiments and still more by the Government's taxation, Capital was tending to draw together its forces and to prepare for a pitched battle. There were many employers who, like Lord Devonport in the strike of the transport workers against the Port of London Authority in 1912, regarded all attempts at conciliation as futile, and desired to fight it out. Since Labour was inclined to be truculent in its demands, Capital followed suit in its answers. There was a good deal of futile talk of " smashing " the workers' organisations before they had become too powerful, and in every dispute there appeared a new intransigence and bitterness. In a time of perfect peace industry seemed to be massing for a conflict, and already the metaphors of war were freely used.

Side by side with this class war had appeared the

beginnings of a sex war. The illogical exclusion oɪ
women from votes had long been the subject of a
decorous agitation which had effected nothing.
Private members' bills on the subject were respect-
fully discussed, and ruthlessly shelved. Now the
advocates of women's suffrage took to militant
methods, and to their unanswerable dialectic added
an attempt to make unworkable the government
machine in which they had no part. These years
furnished a spectacle of both heroism and folly, which,
if it did not persuade an unsympathetic Cabinet,
went far to make its life unbearable. No political
meeting, no occasion of public ceremonial, was safe
from the Suffragists' interruptions, often farcical, but
sometimes tragic. The cause found willing martyrs,
and the hunger strikes of imprisoned women gave
the Home Secretary an insoluble problem.

There has rarely been a more devoted body of
agitators, and those who represented them as mainly
neurotics and degenerates were far from the mark.
The general emancipation of the sex and its admission
to the universities and the professions had brought
to the suffrage cause women of great ability and high
attainments. Moreover, as the conflict continued, a
curious thing happened ; many women, who either
detested militancy or cared nothing for the question,
found themselves insensibly drawn by a kind of sex
loyalty into sympathy. The result was the same as
in industry ; great bodies of human beings were
slowly massed into opposition. At the time it seemed
a terrible thing, but it had its value for the future.
Who shall say that the discipline of the labour
struggles did not do something to equip the British
soldier for the field of battle, and the suffrage crusade

train in self-reliance the many thousands of women who wrought so nobly in the War ?

There was as little peace in Parliament as in the country. Mr. Lloyd George had indeed during the Conference of 1911 been in favour of a patriotic coalition Ministry, from which, if it would increase its usefulness, he was willing to be excluded. But with the breakdown of the Conference, party spirit revived in all its fury. In November of that year, Mr. Balfour, whose detachment had drawn much criticism from his followers, resigned the Conservative leadership, and was succeeded by Mr. Bonar Law, a middle-aged business man, who had never held Cabinet office. The change was not likely to increase the amenities of debate, for Mr. Bonar Law had none of Mr. Balfour's urbanity, and on the major issue of Irish Home Rule he had the passionate convictions of a Scots Covenanter.

Home Rule was not the only anxiety of harassed Ministers. A bill to disestablish the Welsh Church, an old Liberal promise, was introduced in April 1912, and excited impassioned controversy and dismal forebodings ; forebodings happily to be falsified by events, for the disestablished Church in Wales, under wise leadership, was to enter upon a fresh youth. The Insurance Act did not come into effect without many anxious moments for its projectors. In order to get the benefit of the Parliament Act for its measures the Government was compelled to work the House of Commons hard, and Parliament sat continuously from February 14th 1912 to March 7th 1913, with only two months of a summer recess. The Opposition, with the Lords now in shackles and the Commons dragooned under a strict time-table, had some reason

62

to complain that representative Government had become a farce, and that Parliament existed only to register the decrees of an autocratic Cabinet. There was a hair-trigger to the temper of both sides, and explosions and disorderly scenes were sadly frequent.

Nothing revealed the new bitterness in politics so clearly as the Marconi case, which in the autumn of 1912 blew up with the suddenness of a desert sandstorm. The Government were engaged in contracting with the Marconi Company for the creation of a chain of wireless stations. There was a rumour that Ministers had been dealing in Marconi shares, and it required a libel action against a French newspaper to make it clear that there had been no such speculation. What came out, however, was that three Ministers, the Attorney-General, the Chancellor of the Exchequer and the Chief Whip, had received private information which encouraged them to invest in the American Marconi Company, a corporation which had no connection with the English one. The source of this information was the managing director of the English company. These Ministers, therefore, by accepting a tip from its manager, had put themselves under an obligation to a company which had with their Government a contract not yet settled, and still liable to be reviewed by two of the Ministers in their official capacity. The rumours grew so fierce that Mr. Asquith was compelled to appoint a committee to inquire both into the desirability of the contract and the conduct of the three Ministers. The committee reported in June 1913, and on the personal question announced that " all the Ministers concerned have acted throughout in the sincere belief that there was nothing in their action which would in any way conflict with their duty as Ministers of the Crown." An Opposition motion in the House, condemning the want of frankness of the three, was easily defeated, and Mr. Asquith, in summing up, acquitted his colleagues of having infringed any " rules of obligation," but considered that they had not fully observed the " rules of prudence "—which was indeed the common sense of the matter.

This " wretched subject," as Mr. Balfour called it, is only worthy of mention as an example of a change in the standards both of controversy and of conduct. It was obvious that there had been no corruption, but equally obvious that there had been indiscretion. Yet the Opposition in the press and on the platform talked as if Britain were back in the worst days of the eighteenth century, and, more excusably, made play with the new order of the Little Brothers of the Rich, the spectacle of Ministers who had made a speciality of attacks upon idle wealth suddenly appearing among the candidates for that status. The Government's supporters were equally extreme, declaring that there had been not only no corrupt motive, but no improper conduct, and one egregious newspaper announced that Mr. Lloyd George's behaviour had in some mysterious way " sweetened and ennobled public life." Some members of the Liberal party were gravely shocked by the whole business, and the gloss of earnest piety, with which Mr. Gladstone had once endowed their creed, was now patchy and tarnished. But to the great majority of the people it seemed a storm in a tea-cup—which was in itself a proof that private and public standards had declined. Fifty years before the Ministers concerned, however innocent their motives, would have found

their careers at an end. Men had forgotten the
words of Halifax the Trimmer : " An honest man
must lose so many occasions of getting that the world
will scarcely allow him the character of an able one."

III

The irritation caused by the new taxes and the
insurance scheme, and the impotent bitterness
aroused by the Parliament Act, came to a head in
April 1912, when Mr. Asquith introduced an Irish
Home Rule Bill on Mr. Gladstone's model. It
differed from its predecessor in having more of a
federal colour, being according to the Prime Minister
only the first step in a comprehensive system of
devolution for the whole United Kingdom. During
the drafting of the Bill there was some talk of excluding
the Protestant counties of Ulster for a certain number
of years, but it was finally decided to omit this
provision and to keep it as an ultimate bargaining
counter. The measure was hotly debated for the
better part of a year and did not pass its third reading
till January 16th 1913. A fortnight later it was
rejected by the Lords.

At first the line of the Conservative party was
opposition to Home Rule of any kind for any part of
Ireland. On this all sections of the party had always
been agreed, and that summer took place the final
fusion of the Conservative and Unionist wings. But
there was an increasing number of federalists in its
ranks, and had the Irish question been made part
of a reasoned scheme of devolution there might
well have been a split. Many of the younger men

65

recognised the cumbrousness of the existing machine of government, and the need, while there was still the chance, of satisfying Catholic Ireland, the more so as it was clear that a new generation of Irishmen might soon fret under the old Nationalist leadership and follow darker counsels. The reason why the Cabinet, most of them federalists, did not attempt the larger scheme was the same as that which prevented them from essaying the reform of the House of Lords—the matter was too difficult and their time was too short.

But one fact kept the Opposition united, and overrode all the other criticisms of an ill-considered and ill-drafted measure. This was the whole-hearted opposition of Protestant Ulster. If Ulster's exclusion from the Bill would be resented by the Nationalists, it was blindingly clear that her inclusion would be stoutly resisted by Ulster. In September 1912 the Ulster Unionists took time by the forelock, and began to recruit an Ulster Volunteer Force. That same month a solemn Covenant was signed by hundreds of thousands, pledging the signatories never to recognise a Home Rule Parliament in Dublin. Of this agitation the leader was Sir Edward Carson, formerly a law officer of the Crown. The Government were invited, and declined, to prosecute him for high treason, to which he would cheerfully have pleaded guilty. In February 1913 Mr. Churchill went to Belfast and could only speak under military protection. Civil war was apparently imminent so soon as the Parliament Act made the new measure law. Mr. Asquith might preach sweet reasonableness, and point out that it was absurd for a minority to dictate to a majority " upon an apprehension that at some future date they might be injured." The taunt fell on deaf ears, both Ulster and British. " I can imagine," Mr. Bonar Law declared, " no length of resistance to which Ulster will go in which I shall not be ready to support her."

The roots of Ulster's suspicion, part racial and part religious, lay deep in history. That suspicion was beyond the reach of argument, since it was intertwined with the soul of a people who were perfectly ready to suffer for their convictions. They would not be put in subjection to another race, which they distrusted as Cromwell had distrusted it, and to a Church which they feared as Cromwell had feared it. If they were to be driven out of their birthright of British citizenship it would only be at the bayonet's point. There could be no question about the grim reality of this resolve, and it was not confined to Ulster. I can remember as a young man, then nursing my first constituency in Scotland, feeling more deeply on the matter than I had ever felt in my life before about a public question. In the Scottish Lowlands there were thousands of signatories of the Ulster Covenant, and many a man there spent his last pre-War Sunday in the study of large-scale maps of County Tyrone. Now, if a serious and law-abiding people decide that a certain policy is so subversive of their principles and so fatal to their future that it must be met by armed revolution, it is usual for a democratic Government to call a halt and find some other way. But if the Government in its turn concludes that such resistance is factious and unreasonable and must be crushed, then it would appear to be its business to arrest the ringleaders and quell the movement. Mr. Asquith's Government

67

did neither. It allowed Ulster to raise and train an efficient army, and it went on with its Home Rule Bill—which was to make the worst of both worlds.

The Opposition could set out a damaging case. This was not the honest attempt at constitutional reform on the lines of devolution, the need of which it was hard to gainsay. It was an ancient Liberal scheme, in which till the year before Liberals seemed to have lost interest. It had been revived only as part of the Budget bargain. It had never been directly put before the electorate, for the last election had been fought on the House of Lords question with echoes of the Budget. It could not be maintained that Britain as a whole had spoken with a clear voice, and yet it was for this antique relic, most inadequately sanctioned, that the Government proposed to run the risk of civil war.

Ministers could only reply that the deferring of Ireland's hopes would not lead to peace, but they were conscious of the extreme difficulty of the situation, and all the year 1913 was spent in private efforts to negotiate. Unhappily both sides had begun by stating their case so intransigently that compromise was difficult. The King laboured to bring them together ; in the early autumn Lord Curzon and Mr. Bonar Law were at Balmoral, and later the Prime Minister had conversations with the latter and with Mr. John Redmond and Sir Edward Carson. Mr. Redmond saw great difficulties in the exclusion of Ulster, but he was prepared to give her local autonomy and privileged representation in the new Irish Parliament. Sir Edward Carson and Mr. Bonar Law were determined upon exclusion at the start, at any rate, of the four north-east counties as well as Tyrone and Fermanagh. To this Mr. Redmond at first would not agree, but before the end of the year he was willing to allow the Protestant Ulster counties to exclude themselves by plebiscite for a term of years. Sir Edward Carson, who on the matter was at once shrewder and more conciliatory than Mr. Bonar Law, required that no inclusion should be contemplated at any date except under some general scheme of devolution sponsored by the Imperial Parliament. By the end of the year something had been gained, in that the question was no longer a blank negation of Home Rule in any form, but the exclusion from the scheme of Ulster or some part of it, permanently or for a time. The atmosphere was clearer, and the outlook had at least a ray of hope.

The King had played a large part in these attempts at compromise, and the narrowing of the question was largely his doing, for he had patiently striven to present to each side the difficulties of the other. He had cause to be anxious, for he saw looming before him a crisis far graver than the Parliament Act. Correspondents everywhere were appealing to him to use his royal power, and the leaders of the Opposition were turning their eyes to the prerogative. Mr. Bonar Law considered that the King had the right to dismiss his present Ministers and force a dissolution so that the will of the nation could be ascertained. Lord Lansdowne held that, since the Parliament Act had destroyed the power of the Lords to compel an election, that power was now vested only in the Crown, which could either force a dissolution or decree a referendum. Mr. Balfour thought that the King had a right to insist on an election in order to consult the country, and that the country would appreciate such a course. This was also the view of lawyers like Professor Dicey and Sir William Anson. Lord Rosebery, on the other hand, believed that for the King to refuse his assent to the Home Rule Bill, for which he had no personal responsibility, would be a breach of constitutional practice.

Mr. Asquith's views were fully stated in a memorandum which he wrote that September :

A constitutional monarch . . . is entitled and bound to give his Ministers all relevant information which comes to him ; to point out objections which seem to him valid against the course which they advise ; to suggest (if he thinks fit) an alternative policy. . . . But in the end the Sovereign always acts upon the advice which Ministers, after full deliberation and (if need be) reconsideration, feel it their duty to offer. They give that advice well knowing that they can, and probably will, be called to account for it by Parliament.

After pointing out that the only departure from this rule for 130 years had been the request by William IV for the resignation of Lord Melbourne—a disastrous precedent which Queen Victoria had always refused to follow—he continued :

Nothing can be more important, in the best interests of the Crown and of the country, than that a practice, so long established and so well justified by experience, should remain unimpaired. It frees the occupant of the Throne from all personal responsibility for the acts of the Executive and the Legislature. . . . If . . . the king were to intervene on one side, or in one case—which he could only do by dismissing Ministers in *de facto* possession of a parliamentary majority—he would be expected to do the same on another occasion and perhaps for the other side. Every Act of Parliament of the first order of importance, and only passed after acute controversy, would be regarded as bearing the personal *imprimatur* of the Sovereign.

He would, whether he wished it or not, be dragged into the arena of party politics.

Words could not express more clearly the normal constitutional practice of Britain. But the Prime Minister's statement did not exhaust the question. It was conceivable that a Government, placed in power by an election on a different issue, might attempt some measure which offended the great majority of the nation. What if such a measure were certain to lead to civil war ? Edmund Burke had written : " I see no other way but the interposition of the body of the people itself, whenever it shall appear, by some flagrant and notorious act, by some capital innovation, that these representatives are going to overleap the fences of the law and establish an arbitrary power." Might it not be the duty of the King, as the trustee of the people, in such a desperate case to use the prerogative and permit this popular interposition ? Mr. Balfour thought so, and he was a sober councillor with a nice perception of constitutional points. The personal responsibility would be terrible, the risk to the prestige of the Throne incalculable, but might it not be right to face that risk rather than the calamity of a mutinous army and a war between citizens ? It was a graver problem than any sovereign had had to face for two hundred years. Small wonder that the King was assiduous in his labours for peace.

IV

During 1912 and 1913 the other main concern of Ministers, the situation abroad, became more tangled and menacing than ever. Italy fought Turkey over Tripoli ; Greece, Bulgaria, Serbia, and Montenegro allied themselves against a crumbling Turkey and won a victory : the conquerors quarrelled over the division of the loot, the other allies flew at Bulgaria's throat, and Bulgaria was left angry and despoiled. The settlement after these Balkan wars was, in Sir Edward Grey's words, " not one of justice but of force," and it left a store of troubles for the future. The British Foreign Minister did his best to prevent the mischief spreading by calling a conference of the Ambassadors of the Powers, which sat in London from December 1912 to August 1913. The immediate danger was averted, but the Treaty of Bucharest left an open wound in south-eastern Europe. Austria's hopes of a port in the Ægean had received a final blow, and a new and formidable Slav Power now stood in the way of Germany's *Drang nach Osten*, with behind it Russia, the protector of the Slav peoples.

The situation drew Germany, still sore over Morocco, to reflect most seriously upon her position. She saw the various avenues to world-power, on which she had formed her plans, rapidly closing up. The Near East might soon be shut by the new Slav renaissance ; the Far East was too dangerous with Japan at its door ; South America was barred to her adventures by the United States, and most of the rest of the world by Britain. Her navy had come to maturity—it now stood second in the world—and was eager to win laurels. She was already the greatest military Power on earth. She saw the Triple Entente solidifying into an alliance, an alliance accompanied by a steady growth of sympathy and good will. She was afraid of Britain's naval strength and the twenty million addition to Britain's naval estimates ; to her, as a World Power, it seemed intolerable that any single nation should be so omnipotent at sea. She did not appreciate the necessities of an island, administering a world-wide Empire, and read ambition into schemes based only on administrative needs and the desire for a decent security. To Germany it appeared that her neighbours sought to isolate her, to ring her round with hostile alliances and then overwhelm her with the weight of an armed coalition. Her forward policy, entered upon under the impulse of national self-confidence, began now to quicken its pace under the spur of baseless but not wholly unnatural fears.

Early in 1912 Lord Haldane, who had left the War Office for the Woolsack, paid a private visit to Berlin at the request of Sir Edward Grey. He met the Emperor, the Imperial Chancellor, Admiral von Tirpitz and others, and went fully into the whole international situation and all possible matters of dispute. Throughout his difficult task he played the part of a conciliatory but faithful British envoy, jealous alike for his country's interests and his country's honour. He stood out stiffly against Tirpitz for a modification of the German naval programme as a guarantee of good faith. He was scrupulously loyal to Britain's unwritten obligations to France, and kept in close touch with M. Jules Cambon, the French ambassador. A provisional agreement was reached on many points, but on two there could be no settlement. Germany was resolute to proceed with her new naval programme, and the magnitude of the increases provided for made it impossible for Britain to do otherwise than lay down two ships to

73

her one. On that matter our attitude could not be compromise, but watchful competition. Again, Germany insisted, as the basis for an understanding, upon a formula of Britain's unconditional neutrality in the event of a European War, to which Britain could not assent without a betrayal of France. The conference ended with expressions of friendship, but without much practical result, though undoubtedly it did something to clear the air.

Lord Haldane returned home with a divided mind. There were many things to disquiet him—the personality of Tirpitz, the spirit of the General Staff, the character of the latest German naval law ; above all, the unconditional neutrality formula. On the other hand, he believed that the Emperor and his civilian Ministers sincerely desired peace in their then mood, and there is reason to think that in the spring of 1912 this was true. Lord Haldane and his colleagues came to a definite conclusion as to their immediate policy. They must avoid any pinpricks, and any blowing of warning trumpets in Britain, for these would be misconstrued in Germany, and would strengthen the hands of those who clamoured for war. By judicious quiescence on their part the Imperial Faustus might be prevented from making a bargain with the devil. Such a decision was acceptable to a Government perplexed and a little weary. It was acceptable to the Prime Minister, in whose philosophy of life the doctrine of a " friendly Universe " held a conspicuous place, and who considered that most political questions, if left alone, would settle themselves. It was acceptable to Sir Edward Grey, whose success as a conciliator had inclined him to the belief that patience and good humour would tide over the worst

times.   On the information then at their disposal the
decision was natural and right.

But, so far as we can read the dark riddle of these
years in Germany, in 1913 there came a change of
mood, which British Ministers did not diagnose.
Their minds were monopolised by their difficulties
at home, and the whole political atmosphere prevented any close attention to the creeping shadows
and broken lights of the European situation.   That
year saw the completion of the first quarter-century
of the Emperor's reign, and the celebrations, with
their awakening of historic memories, sent a sudden
surge of pride through the German people.   The
time had come to make a settlement with rivals not
by the slow methods of diplomacy, but by the
summary power of the sword.   It was the year of
the new German army law, and every military chief,
from the younger Moltke downward, was busy with
arrogant defiances to the world.   As early as April
the French Government received a secret report
setting forth the purpose for which the swollen army
of Germany was to be used at the appropriate
moment.   In November the Emperor told the King
of the Belgians at Potsdam that he looked upon war
with France as inevitable and close at hand.   About
the same time M. Jules Cambon warned his Government that the balance had now clearly swung to the
side of the war party, and that the Emperor would
not resist them.   Fear of Russia was perhaps the
chief motive ; the Austrian Conrad von Hoetzendorff
had been pressing the need for the " great solution "
on the German Staff, and the Emperor was a convert
to an " inevitable war between East and West."

No exact date can be fixed for this momentous

change. It was no doubt a gradual process, at first a subtle altering of outlook and perspective which slowly drew to a conscious policy. So far as we can judge the Emperor's mind, he did not then conceive of the coming conflict as a world conflagration ; Britain would stand out—on that point Germany, plentifully supplied with the reports of secret agents, was positive ; France would speedily be broken ; after some sullen fighting in the East the Slav peril would be checked ; Germany would emerge as indisputably the greatest of the Powers, heavy indemnities would pay her bills, and her mailed diplomacy would not be denied in future conclaves of the peoples.

It was the decision primarily of the army and navy chiefs, whose influence with Emperor and nation far outweighed that of the civilian ministers. But there were many elements in the new Germany on which it could count for support. There was the Prussian squirearchy which had made the army ; there were the new kings of trade whom success had smitten with megalomania ; there were the theorists who from Treitschke had learned a strange doctrine of history and from Nietzsche a perverted philosophy of life. There was no great dæmonic figure who imposed his creed upon the people ; the preceptors were for the most part excited mediocrities ; but there was deadly peril in the conjunction of a flamboyant Emperor ambitious of ranking with the makers of history, an army and a navy burning to prove their prowess to the world, an aristocracy intolerant of all democratic ideals, rulers of industry at once exultant and nervous, popular teachers preaching a gospel of race arrogance, and throughout the nation a vague half-mystical striving towards a new destiny.

The British Government, faced with a risk of war which was not yet a certainty, were bound to take no steps to insure that certainty. The most that can be said in criticism of them is that too many sedatives were applied to the national mind. For example, Lord Roberts's scheme for national training, impossible as it may have been, was repelled by the ordinary Government apologist with arguments that were foolish except on the assumption that the age of Saturn had returned. One thing, however, was efficiently done. The Haldane regime at the War Office had produced an army as perfect for its size as any in the world ; the latest German navy bill forced Britain proportionately to expand and equip her Fleet. That Fleet, by an arrangement with France, was concentrated in home waters, and the new maritime front was the North Sea. There was a great naval assembly in the spring of 1912 at Portland, when for four days the King abode among his sailors. Mr. Churchill, whose post was now the most vital in the Government, made the Admiralty yacht his office and his home.

The increased naval estimates for 1914 were strongly opposed by a section of the Cabinet, and for a month it seemed as if the First Lord must resign. Even for this, our traditional first line of defence, it was hard to get proper attention, since their opponents had always made a specialty of it, and in the embittered state of party feeling to appear to agree with the Opposition seemed to many of the Government followers a betrayal of principles. Yet all the time the weightier members of the Cabinet had in their

77

hearts the knowledge that behind the crudities of
their critics there was much deadly truth, and
that at any moment what they labelled as scare-
mongering might be terribly justified as foresight.
Mr. Lloyd George, " forgetting the bright speed
he bore " at the Mansion House in the Agadir
crisis, joined the ranks of the prophets of smooth
things. On January 3rd 1914, in a press interview,
he deplored the folly of outlay on armaments, with
special reference to naval expenditure, praised the
unaggressive temper of Germany, declared that the
prospects of the world never had been more peaceful,
and implored Liberalism not to betray its trust.

v

After his return from India the King was at the
disposal of his subjects for those ceremonial duties
traditionally associated with the Throne. Buckingham
Palace, once the dingiest object in London, had its
façade reconstructed and no longer shamed the
dignity of St. James's Park. There were a few big
functions, like the Windsor garden party in the
summer of 1912, and the State banquet to President
Poincaré in June 1913, when the King spoke
eloquently of " l'esprit de confiance et de franchise
mutuelles avec laquel la France et la Grande-
Bretagne ont abordé ces divers problèmes." In May
1913 their Majesties visited Berlin, where they were
well received, and the King had luncheon with the
officers corps of the dragoon regiment which bore
Queen Victoria's name and of which he was colonel-
in-chief. But for the most part his work lay in getting

into touch with the varied activities of his people. He visited ancient schools and new universities ; he had a long tour in South Wales, where he laid the foundation stone of the new National Museum of Wales at Cardiff ; he saw something of the mining areas, both north and south ; he paid a week's visit to Lancashire, after a tour of the Potteries ; he laid the foundation stone of the new London County Hall. He had his father's concern for the work of the great municipalities and especially for their housing schemes. In these tasks—a new form of royal progress—he gained an insight into aspects of the nation's life to which few politicians attain. He had a quick and catholic interest in all human activities, he made friends readily, and, having a tenacious memory, he did not forget what he heard and saw.

For the rest, the life of the Court was a peaceful enclave to which the eyes of his subjects could turn with comfort. It was simple and homelike and very close to their own. In 1912 the Prince of Wales entered Magdalen College like any other under-graduate, very different from his grandfather's secluded and pedestalled university career. The King shared fully in the interests and tastes of the ordinary man. His chief relaxation was shooting ; he was one of the two or three best shots in England —the first monarch since Charles II who had been in the first rank in a field sport. It was a Court without courtiers. The King had no favourites, no inner circle of the privileged, but he had a thousand attached friends.

There was need of some such cool and orderly background in England, for in those years there was a fevered spirit abroad. The internal-combustion

79   F

engine had speeded up the pace of life. The old
horse-bus had disappeared from the streets, and
motor-cars or motor-bicycles were now common in
every class. London had become notably noisier and
less attractive to quiet people. The first stages had
been won in the conquest of the air, and in 1913
M. Pégoud was " looping the loop " and giving the
world a new notion of what air stability meant. The
defence services had to adjust their ideas ; motors
were beginning to replace horse-transport in the
army, the immense importance of the submarine was
being slowly understood, and in the beginning of
1912 Lord Fisher was writing to Mr. Churchill, " For
God's sake trample on and stamp out protected
Cruisers and hurry up Aviation." In society the
financier was more popular than he deserved to be,
and the parade of luxury had increased and the craze
for quickly-won wealth. There was everywhere a
kind of comfortless excitement, a vulgarity of outlook,
a coarsening of fibre, and what looked to old-
fashioned people like a weakening of stamina. The
Russian ballet had popularised new types of dancing,
and from America came rag-time music, and from
outlandish places various uncouth forms of motion.
In the ball-room a novel type of young man appeared,
with lank hair plastered back from a lean brow. I
remember in 1913 a French visitor calling my
attention to them, and quoting Falstaff's " cankers
of a calm world and a long peace."

It was a world formally at peace but with no ease,
a world without strong faiths or inspirations, confident,
but with its confidence often nervously cracking.
Now and then something happened to " tease us out
of thought." The sinking of the *Titanic* in April

1912 showed that Nature, which we thought we had shackled, could turn in her bonds and make sport of us. And the news which came to England early next year of the death of Captain Scott and his comrades in the Antarctic wastes, a failure more glorious than any victory, reminded us, almost with a shock, of that virtue which is the chief end of man.

CHAPTER IV

DESCENSUS AVERNI

THE first seven months of 1914 saw the British nation living like some prosperous settlement on the glacis of a volcano—a merry and full life with a background of creeping fears. One part of the volcanic skirts was already shaken with tremors, and to this anxious eyes were turned when a preoccupied people had leisure for thought. But another part was in the mind only of the few. This had threatened danger in the past, but it was for the moment quiescent, and only an occasional muttering told of the hidden fires. But these few understood only too well how thin was the crust, and how at any moment it might be rent by chaos and death.

I

The immediate preoccupation was Ireland. Ulster had organised a provisional Government, to come into force if the Home Rule Bill became law, and a volunteer army to resist coercion. Arms were being imported, and men were drilling in every parish. This challenge could not be ignored by the Nationalists, and a similar activity was soon afoot in Dublin. Mr. Redmond believed that the best policy was to let Ulster alone, in the hope that the trouble would blow over, for he feared that any coercion of the north would wake in the south new forces of disorder, of whose power he was already cognisant and which he knew that he could not control. The British Government accepted his advice the more readily as the discussions of the previous year had shown them that the Ulster leader was no irresponsible rebel.

Sir Edward Carson, himself not an Ulsterman, had begun his crusade in the hope that Ulster's resistance would kill Home Rule for the whole island. He had been an impenitent die-hard on the House of Lords question, and would have accepted the creation of new peers, because he believed that it might lead to a reformed Upper House, and that any such chamber would make the Government's Home Rule scheme impossible. His policy was for Ireland as a whole, not for a province. But as the months passed he became convinced that Ulster's problem must be taken as a thing by itself, and that the best tactics were to insist upon her exclusion from the Bill. On this point the Cabinet had shown itself willing to treat, and the dispute was now a question of details. He was proving himself much less intransigent, as he was much less rhetorical, than the non-Irish Conservative leaders, for he realised, as few Ministers realised, that our decorous British democracy had elements in it of peril and surprise, and that sleeping dogs were being roused which it was better to let lie.

But in the early spring one of these dogs stirred uneasily. If no agreement was reached and Ulster in fact rebelled, coercion might follow, as it had followed half a century before in the American Civil War. The instrument of such coercion must be the British Army. What was likely to be the temper of that Army? There was already acute anxiety among many officers, and it was decided—wisely enough—that, if the Army had to be used against the Ulster volunteers, officers with an Ulster domicile should be excused service without prejudice to their professional careers. Now began a series of disastrous blunders. It was obviously necessary to take steps to protect stores and munitions in the disaffected areas, and the measures adopted for the purpose were needlessly inflammatory. Mr. Churchill arranged that the forthcoming practice of one of the battle squadrons should take place off the island of Arran, which is not very far from Belfast Lough. Wild rumours reached the House of Commons, and on March 19th, in the debate on a vote of censure, Sir Edward Carson declared that the Government were mobilising troops for coercion, and walked out of the House; while Mr. Bonar Law laid down the doctrine that in a case of mere disorder the Army must obey, but that in a civil war soldiers were citizens like other people. Next day that happened at the Curragh which put a match to the tinder.

Sir Arthur Paget, the Commander-in-Chief in Ireland, summoned his officers and assured them that permission would be given in certain contingencies for officers domiciled in Ulster to " disappear," a concession already familiar in the Indian Army. But he went further; he told the rest that, if they were not willing to carry out any duties assigned to them, they must say so at once and be dismissed. The natural assumption was that officers were being ordered to express their views on Government policy, and to declare their willingness to serve against Ulster or to leave the service. Brigadier-General

Hubert Gough and fifty-seven of his colleagues of the 3rd Cavalry Brigade accepted their dismissal.

The fat was now fairly in the fire. There was a cry of mutiny among the Government followers, but there could be no mutiny in men accepting one of the alternatives put before them by their superiors. The Cabinet had been imperfectly advised about the whole business, and so great was the muddle that the King had not been informed at all. General Gough and the others were summoned to London and the situation explained to them, after which they returned to their duties. A Cabinet memorandum, issued later as an Army order, laid it down that " no officer or soldier should in future be questioned by his superior officer as to the attitude he will adopt, or as to his action, in the event of his being required to obey orders dependent on future or hypothetical contingencies," and that " an officer or soldier is forbidden in future to ask for assurances as to orders which he may be required to obey." The Prime Minister took his stand on the principle laid down by the elder Pitt during the Jacobite Rising of 1745. " The right of inquiring what measures may conduce to the advantage and security of the public belongs not to the Army but to this House. . . . Our armies have no better right to determine for themselves than any other body of men, nor are we to suffer them to prescribe laws to the legislature, or to govern those by whose authority they subsist."

But the chapter of blunders was not ended. Colonel Seely, the Secretary of State for War, in forwarding this memorandum to General Gough, added two paragraphs on his own account, one of which declared that the Government had no intention of using the

forces of the Crown " to crush political opposition
to the policy or principles of the Home Rule Bill,"
and the addendum was initialled by Sir John French,
the Chief of the Imperial General Staff, and by the
Adjutant-General. This, in Liberal, Labour and
Nationalist eyes, was selling the pass with a vengeance.
Colonel Seely and the two soldiers resigned, and
Mr. Asquith himself took on the War Office. The
debates in the Commons during March were bitter
and confused, the Prime Minister repeating his refusal
to permit the entrance of " hypothetical contingencies " into a soldier's duties, and Labour members
pointing out gleefully what an excellent precedent
it all afforded for the next industrial dispute. The
hidden fires were beginning to crackle.

They crackled more noisily in the following weeks.
At the end of April there was a great gun-running
on the Ulster coast, when, with the assistance of
12,000 men, 25,000 rifles and 3,000,000 cartridges
were landed and distributed. Police proceedings
were useless, for no jury would convict. There was a
violent scene in the House of Commons on May 21st,
when the third reading of the Home Rule Bill was
moved. After it was carried Sir Edward Carson left
for Belfast " to make arrangements for the final
scene." It was known that in southern Ireland there
was already a fighting force of 100,000 volunteers.

If it was a difficult time for Ministers, it was more
difficult for the King. He was head of the Army,
and the Curragh incident had revealed to him that
the partition had worn thin between order and
anarchy. He was being urged from every side to
intervene, to refuse the royal assent to the Home
Rule Bill, to appeal himself to the nation, to avert

at any cost civil war. Throughout the agitation he
had kept a cool head, and had been untiring in his
efforts for peace. But few men have ever been in a
harder position, and there was pathos in his quota-
tion, in a letter to Mr. Asquith at the beginning of
June, of a sentence from his Coronation message :
" Whatever perplexities or difficulties may be before
me and my people, we shall all unite in facing them
resolutely, calmly, and with public spirit, confident
that, under divine guidance, the ultimate outcome
may be to the common good."

He made one last effort to achieve this hope, and
gladly acceded to the Prime Minister's request that
he should summon in his own name a conference
of the party-leaders at Buckingham Palace. Only
two points of controversy remained : the exact size
of the excluded Ulster, and the terms on which a
future union with the rest of Ireland might be effected.
There were eight members of the Conference—the
Prime Minister and Mr. Lloyd George for the Government, Lord Lansdowne and Mr. Bonar Law for the
Opposition, Mr. Redmond and Mr. Dillon for the
Nationalists, and Sir Edward Carson and Captain
Craig for Ulster. For the second time in four years
the King had called into council others besides his
official advisers. The Conference held only four
sittings, and on July 24th its failure was announced
to the world. Two days after there was a big gun-
running at Howth, near Dublin, which involved a
conflict with British regular troops. The Home Rule
Bill must become law at once in order to take advantage of the Parliament Act. When that moment
arrived it seemed that nothing but a miracle could
prevent civil war.

A world earthquake was to forestall a local landslide. Would that landslide have come if the greater
shock had not intervened ? I find it hard to believe
it. Both of the parties in the dispute had allowed
themselves to be manœuvred into a position where
concession was difficult. But the ultimate core of
difference had become ludicrously small—a few
parishes in County Tyrone, and certain provisions
about the future. It is true that most of the great
contests of history have been fought on fine points
and narrow margins, but these points and margins
have been matters of principle, not of detail. Mr.
Asquith's intention was to pass concurrently with the
Bill an amending measure which would allow the
disputed counties to vote themselves in or out, and
would drop the proposal for Ulster's automatic inclusion under a Dublin Parliament after a term of years.
Moreover, he would have announced that after a
short winter session the Government would go to
the country early in 1915.

It is difficult to believe that Sir Edward Carson,
who was by far the most powerful agent in the matter,
would have allowed things to proceed to extremities.
He had shown himself the most conciliatory of his
party. He was well aware that the success of his
cause depended largely on how it was regarded by
the people of Britain. He was not forgetful of the
solemn appeal which the King had made when he
summoned the Conference :

We have in the past endeavoured to act as a civilising example
to the world, and to me it is unthinkable, as it must be to you,
that we should be brought to the brink of fratricidal strife upon
issues apparently so capable of adjustment as those you are now
asked to consider, if handled in a spirit of generous compromise.

Had there been no world war, it seems likely that,

chance, for which she had been waiting, of removing once and for all the Slav menace. Her General Staff had long had an understanding with the German Staff, which provided for co-operation in a war in which the opponents were envisaged as Russia and France. Berlin encouraged her in making demands on Serbia, which Serbia could not accept without ceasing to be a nation, and this with full appreciation of the fact that Russia could not stand aside. A dispatch from the German Ambassador in Vienna was annotated by the German Emperor, " Now or never." At a meeting at Potsdam on July 5th, a letter was read from the Emperor Franz Joseph, and Germany promised Austria support in whatever course she pursued. In Vienna Count Berchtold had his way, and the warnings of the far abler Count Tisza were disregarded. With the cognisance of Germany an impossible Note was presented to Belgrade, at a moment when there were domestic troubles in each of the nations of the Triple Entente and their diplomatic machines were out of gear. Serbia, having consulted Russia, went to the extreme limit of complaisance, accepting all Austria's demands, with two reservations, on which she asked for a reference to the Hague Tribunal. But the Austrian Note was in the nature of a rhetorical question : it did not expect an answer. Forty-five minutes after an unsatisfactory reply was received the Austrian Minister left Belgrade. On July 28th Austria declared war.

The consequences that followed were as startling and inevitable as the explosions which attend the firing of a powder train. Russia could not look on unmoved, and on the 29th ordered a partial mobilisation. Germany, determined on some kind of war, but anxious to limit it if possible, and unwilling to drop the mask of reasonableness, made a parade of peace-making. It is needless to trace the steps in these clumsy manœuvres which deceived nobody. The soldiers were in charge, and there could be no going back. In Russia partial mobilisation was followed by a general one ; Germany mobilised in turn and sent Russia an ultimatum ; France was compelled to follow the example of her ally. By the end of the month Austria was at war with Serbia, and Germany, France and Russia were waiting to march. Mobilisation is the first step in a campaign, and Germany from long preparation was in that game far ahead of her rivals ; she could afford to wait, for her well-oiled machine moved fast. The question of the responsibility for the War will no doubt be debated for many years, but certain facts stand out clear in the mists of ingenious dialectic. Austria was the immediate cause, but the spur behind her was Germany. As for personalities, Berchtold and Conrad in Austria must bear the chief blame, and in Germany the army and navy chiefs. The German civilian statesmen were negligible, and the Emperor a bombastic echo of stronger men.

But it is with Britain that we are concerned. The burden in that last week lay especially upon two men, the Foreign Secretary and the Prime Minister, who was now also Secretary of State for War. Sir Edward Grey, to whom the duty of first action fell, had two purposes—to persuade the Powers concerned to come into conference, and to keep Britain's liberty of ultimate decision uncompromised. There must be no risk of our drifting blindly into war. He had three convictions : that a general European war

under modern conditions would be an unthinkable
disaster; that Germany, who controlled Austria,
had the key of the situation; that, if war came and
France was involved, Britain dare not stand aside.

His first step was to approach Germany, France
and Italy with a view to calling a conference in
London to mediate in the Austro-Serbian quarrel.
It was perhaps a blunder that Austria was not included in the invitation. From Paris and Rome he
received a cordial response, from Berlin a flat refusal.
He returned to the charge, and proposed that, if
the principle of mediation were accepted, Germany
herself should suggest the lines on which it should be
conducted. On the 28th Bethmann-Hollweg, the
Imperial Chancellor, sent for the British Ambassador
and told him that a conference was impossible, since
it would look like sitting in judgment on sovereign
Powers, but that he was anxious for peace, and was
advising Vienna to negotiate directly with Petrograd.
Next day Sir Edward Grey very seriously and
courteously warned Prince Lichnowsky of the
dangerous road Germany was walking. "While
[the situation] was restricted to the countries actually
involved, we had no thought of interfering in it.
But if Germany becomes involved in it, and then
France, its area might be so great that it would
involve all European interests; and I did not wish
him to be misled by the friendly tone of our conversations—which I hoped might continue—into thinking
that we should stand aside." It was on a report of
this talk that the Emperor scribbled: "The low
scoundrel! genuinely English!"

On Thursday the 30th arrived Germany's bid for
British neutrality. It was the result of a council at

Potsdam the night before. Provided Britain remained neutral, Germany undertook to seek no territorial gains at the expense of France, at any rate in
Europe ; and as for Belgium, " if she did not side
against Germany, her integrity would also be re-
spected, when the war was over." This meant that
Germany had resolved upon war, and it had an
ominous hint of tampering with Belgium. Sir
Edward Grey replied in words that could not be
misconstrued. He rejected utterly the suggestion
that Britain should bind herself to a disgraceful
neutrality. He appealed once more to Germany
to work with him to preserve the peace of Europe,
and he concluded with the expression of a hope for
a future league of nations, which at the moment
seemed a vague academic notion, but which the
terrors of war were one day to make a reality.

During the next two days Germany disclosed her
hand. The partial mobilisation of Russia, which to
Sir Edward Grey seemed a reasonable defensive
precaution, was treated by her as a hostile act. She
offered France neutrality on insulting terms. She
proposed to Belgium a commercial bargain for the
right to use her territory, which Belgium refused.
For a moment it appeared that Austria was wavering, and Sir Edward Grey saw an eleventh-hour
chance of peace. But by midday on the 31st ulti-
matums had gone from Germany to both Russia and
France ; henceforth the doings of Austria had no
importance, for the conduct of affairs had been taken
into stronger hands.

On the morning of the 31st the British Cabinet
met to consider M. Paul Cambon's appeal for an
assurance that Britain, if war came, would stand by

France's side. The reply was that it could not yet guarantee the intervention of Britain, but must wait for the situation to develop. Sir Edward Grey was uncertain of the attitude of his countrymen. Long insensitiveness to foreign politics had unfitted British opinion to read the signs now written large on the sky. Mr. Bonar Law was doubtful about the views of the Conservative party, and high finance and the extreme Radical press were at one in their determination to avoid war. The Foreign Secretary was not less uncertain about his colleagues. There were perhaps four other men in the Cabinet of his own way of thinking, men who had been specially concerned with foreign or defence questions. But the majority refused to admit the possibility of Britain being involved—a perfectly honourable attitude on the facts before them. It would have been a disgrace had there not been a peace party when the situation was so uncertain. The enforced caution of Britain had no effect on German policy. Had the news of a military alliance between France and Britain been published that day Germany would not, and could not, have swerved one hair's breadth from her plan.

That day the King received a message from the President of the French Republic, who, while admitting that Britain was under no formal obligation, appealed to her to declare herself on France's side as offering the one chance of peace. That chance had already gone, but M. Poincaré's message is proof, if proof were needed, of the earnest desire of France to avert war. The King, after consulting his Ministers, replied on the following morning with the same answer as Sir Edward Grey had already given to M. Cambon. There was still a faint hope of

peace, and till that had departed the pledge asked
for could not be given. But before many hours had
passed that hope had vanished even from the minds
of the British Cabinet.

On Saturday, August 1st, came the German order
for general mobilisation, followed in the afternoon
by France's. War between Germany and Russia began
that evening. The centre of interest now moved to
Belgium. Sir Edward Grey had asked the French
and German governments for a promise that they
would respect Belgium's neutrality so long as no
other Power violated it. France gave the assurance
gladly, but the German reply was disquieting. She
could not answer without " disclosing part of her
plan of campaign in the event of war ensuing " ;
besides, she considered that Belgium had already
committed certain hostile acts. It looked as if the
stage were being set for a new version of the fable
of the Wolf and the Lamb. With this news Sir
Edward Grey attended a meeting of the Cabinet.
The situation was changing and some of the strongest
non-interventionists had begun to waver. Belgium
was clearly threatened, and the question of Belgium
directly touched British interests and British honour.
It was resolved that Germany must be warned that
here lay a plain cause of strife, unless the required
pledge was forthwith given.

The week-end was such as no one then living had
ever known. For so widespread a sense of foundations destroyed and a world turned topsy-turvy we
must go back to the days of the French Revolution.
In Britain it was fortunately the season of the August
Bank Holiday, and, though the Bank rate had risen
to ten per cent., the chaos into which markets were

falling was not widely realised. But an air of great and terrible things impending impressed the most casual spectator. Crowds hung about telegraph offices and railway stations ; men stood in the streets in little groups ; there was not much talking, but long spells of tense silence. The country was uneasy. It dreaded war ; it was beginning to realise the immensity of the crisis ; many feared, too, a dishonourable and improvident peace.

In the broiling weather of Sunday, August 2nd, things marched fast in Europe. Shortly after dawn German troops entered Luxemburg territory, and about the same time German cavalry patrols crossed the Alsace border and had a brush with French pickets. That evening Germany presented her ultimatum to Belgium, demanding a passage for her troops. In London the Cabinet sat from eleven till two, and again in the late afternoon, and revealed much difference of view. But anxiety about Belgium was making converts. Sir Edward Grey was authorised to inform France that if the German fleet came into the Channel or through the North Sea to attack the French ports, the British Navy would give her all the protection in its power. It was a step which in common decency we were bound to take, since France by arrangement with us had depleted her Atlantic and Channel defences and concentrated in the Mediterranean. That day the Opposition leaders, collected hurriedly from distant country houses, sent the Prime Minister a note offering their unqualified support in any step which he might take on behalf of the honour and security of Britain. It was now plain that, if Belgium resisted, our entry into the war was assured.

On the morning of Monday the 3rd, twelve hours after the receipt of the ultimatum, Belgium made her answer. " The Belgian Government, if they were to accept the proposal made to them, would sacrifice the honour of their nation and betray their duty towards Europe. . . . They are firmly resolved to repel by all the means in their power every attack upon their rights." This bold defiance, delivered while Britain still seemed to hesitate, was like the sudden wind that sweeps a morning fog from the valleys. At the same hour King Albert telegraphed to King George making a last appeal for the diplomatic intervention of Britain to safeguard the integrity of his country. But the hour for diplomacy had passed, since the enemy was already marching. When the British Cabinet met that morning it was now unanimous, having shed its dissidents. In Sir Edward Grey's words, we " began all to face the same way, for we had our backs to the same straight wall." Mr. Churchill informed his colleagues that he had taken timely steps, and that the whole sea power of Britain was in readiness for war. An hour before, Lord Haldane, acting for the Prime Minister at the War Office, had ordered the mobilisation of the Army, an act of incalculable importance at a time when every hour was vital.

The views of the House of Commons had still to be ascertained. The day was a Bank Holiday, and that afternoon everywhere in the land crowds waited at post offices for the first news of the Foreign Secretary's speech. His statement was such as only he could have made. It was the expression, in plain words without rhetoric or passion, of a most honest and peace-loving mind, which had left no channel of mediation untried, which had striven against every rebuff to avert calamity, and which now sadly but inevitably was forced towards war. The gist of his speech was, in the words which he wrote later, that " if we did not stand by France and stand up for Belgium against this aggression, we should be isolated, discredited and hated, and there would be before us nothing but a miserable and ignoble future." The House of Commons received his statement with almost unanimous approval. The twelve days had ended when diplomacy had laboured to buttress the tottering barrier. Britain, thanks partly to the wisdom of her leaders, but mainly to chance, faced war with a united government, a united people, and a united Empire.

Ever since that day it has been debated whether an earlier decision on our part might not have averted tragedy. Hypothetics is at its best a barren game, but it is one to which the human mind is prone, when it remembers its fallibility. It is certain that any attempt in the years before 1914 to enlarge the British Army to a continental scale would have precipitated the crisis. What is arguable is that the transformation of the *entente* with France into a defensive alliance, could it have been accomplished peaceably at an earlier date, might have given pause to Germany's ambition. The right answer seems to be that it was not possible in the then mood of the country, and that any Government which had proposed it would have been turned out of office ; the criticism on this score is not of British statesmen but of the British nation.

On the policy of the final month two things may be said. So unprepared was the national mind to contemplate war as a fact, that a declaration that we would stand by France, if made any time before August 3rd, would have split the Cabinet, would have been repudiated by the House of Commons, and would probably not have been accepted by the great majority of the people. Britain had to be educated into a new mood, and it was only the crisis of Belgium which expedited that education. The second thing is that such a declaration would not have altered Germany's purpose one jot. She was in the grip of the military machine which she had fashioned, and whose heavy movement, once it began, could not be checked without a general disruption. She did not believe that Britain's entrance into the War would make much difference. Her civilian statesmen and, intermittently, her Emperor had heavy thoughts, but the monster which they had begot brushed them aside. When at the very end the Emperor would have left Belgium alone and turned his eyes eastward, he was told by Moltke that the advance of armies of millions of men was the result of years of painstaking work and could not possibly be changed. The truth is that the pent-up forces of strife had been weakening the containing walls for a decade, and no last-moment reinforcement could have saved the dam. The War was made by the General Staffs, not of Germany only, with behind them as a propelling force a great weight of popular arrogance and greed and fear; and no action on the part of Britain, a Power outside that sinister community, could have held them back. In all history there is no more solemn warning of the calamity which ensues when the servant becomes the master.

DESCENSUS AVERNI

III

The imagination fastens on the ultimate stage of
the drama, the moments before the storm broke.
The last official acts of Britain were curiously informal. The overrunning of Belgium, which began
on the morning of Tuesday the 4th, had raised a
moral issue which put all political considerations out
of court. The Cabinet left the drafting of the ultimatum to Germany to the Prime Minister and Sir
Edward Grey. Unless a satisfactory reply was given
before midnight the British Ambassador in Berlin
was instructed to ask for his passports.

Every man now in middle life who was then in
England must retain a sharp recollection of how
the War came to him. In my own memory certain
scenes stand out from the blurred impression of
crowded streets and faces hourly growing more
anxious. One is of a dinner of Conservative members
at the House of Commons less than a week before the
climax, when all were sceptical of Britain entering
the War, and one or two well-known politicians were
as firm in their pacifism as any Radical. Another
is of the City, which resembled nothing so much as a
beehive which has been overturned. There were
leaders of finance who fortunately kept their heads and
faced the unknown bravely and calmly, but there
were many distracted prophets of doom, who succeeded in impressing Lord Morley but not the robust
Prime Minister. "The greatest ninnies I ever had
to tackle," Mr. Asquith wrote. "I found them all
in a state of funk like old women chattering over tea-
cups in a cathedral town." Small blame to them,

perhaps, for they saw the structure on which their life's work was based dissolving furiously before their eyes, and could conceive of no possible resurrection.

I have also memories of some of the protagonists : Sir Edward Grey, when I breakfasted with him on the Saturday morning, pale and a little haggard but steadfast as a rock ; Mr. Churchill's high spirits, which sobered now and then when he remembered the desperate issues ; Lord Haldane's uncanny placidity ; Prince Lichnowsky's grey face and tragic eyes. Then, as the hours passed and war became certain, one's friends in the Services disappeared on urgent errands. The Fleet had already moved into the northern solitudes. A man of letters, sailing his boat past the English capes, had a strange vision at dawn.

Like ghosts, like things themselves made out of mist, there passed, between me and the newly risen sun, a procession of great forms, all in line, hastening northward. It was the Fleet recalled. The slight haze along the distant waters had thickened, perhaps, imperceptibly ; or perhaps the great speed of the men-of-war buried them too quickly in the distance. But, for whatever cause, this marvel was of short duration. It was seen for a moment, and in a moment it was gone. Then I knew that war would come, and my mind was changed.*

The mind was changed ; that is the truest description of what happened to the British nation during those ultimate days. People were desperately puzzled ; they could not step, as the French could, immediately into recognition of a catastrophe which had always been at the back of their thoughts. But everyone realised that a great test had come, that Britain had not strayed idly into war, but must meet with clear eyes a challenge which threatened her existence and every decency of life. What would be left at the end of it not only of material comfort but of spiritual health ? Men faced the question according to their

* H. Belloc : *The Cruise of the Nona.*

natures, and the enforced idleness of the Bank Holiday gave opportunity for thought.

One conviction was universal : it was a monstrous hazard about which prediction was futile. To many serious men it seemed like the drawing down of a black curtain on all that was old and happy. Sir Edward Grey, watching from the windows of the Foreign Office the lights springing out in the dusk, said to a friend, " The lamps are going out all over Europe ; we shall not see them lit again in our life-time." Whatever happened, the world would never be the same again, for we were embarking upon untried and uncharted seas. To some, especially young men perplexed and disillusioned by the pre-war confusion, it seemed like the opening of barred doors into a freer air. Many, behind their anxiety, felt almost a sense of relief. The unknown peril which they had so long dreaded had at last taken concrete form, and could be faced and fought. There was a stirring, too, throughout the whole land of national pride, the sense of a common interest knit together again after all the envious rents of party strife, and people drew towards the mystic centre of their unity. On the Sunday night great masses surrounded Buckingham Palace and acclaimed the King and Queen, and the duties of statesmen in Whitehall were per-formed to the accompaniment of echoes, borne across the Park, of the National Anthem and the Marseillaise.

When the British ultimatum arrived in Berlin the Imperial Chancellor was speaking in the Reichstag the historic passage in which he defended his country's action in Belgium by that necessity which is above law. " The wrong—I speak frankly—that we are committing we will try to make good as soon as our military goal is reached. He who is threatened as we are threatened and is fighting for his all can have but the one thought—how he is to hack his way through." In the evening he saw the British Ambassador. He was deeply agitated. "He said that the step taken by His Majesty's Government was terrible to a degree : just for a word—'neutrality,' a word which in war time had so often been disregarded—just for a scrap of paper Great Britain was going to make war on a kindred nation who desired nothing better than to be friends with her." Had Britain considered the price ? he asked excitedly ; to which the Ambassador answered that fear of consequences was not an excuse for breaking solemn engagements. Germany made no formal reply to the ultimatum which expired at midnight. By ten o'clock the news had leaked out, the newsboys in the streets were shouting war with Britain, and presently the crashing of glass in the Embassy windows told that the Berlin mob had awakened to the fact that the strife was not to be confined to the continent of Europe, but was to rage through the wide world. "The British change the whole situation," the Emperor told Mr. Gerard a few days later. "An obstinate nation ! They will keep up the war. It cannot end soon."

In London the last hours passed calmly. "Truth hath a quiet breast." The Prime Minister and Sir Edward Grey sat in the Cabinet room in Downing Street, a silent place except for the far-away singing of the great crowds around the Palace. Big Ben struck eleven—midnight by German time—and War had come. Presently Mr. Churchill arrived from the Admiralty. The war telegram had gone to every ship of the British Navy throughout the world.

PART II

CHAPTER I

CONTACT

I

WAR in older days had been a gladiatorial show in which, in a circumscribed area, a selected manhood fought on a narrow issue. Now it was to cover the whole earth, and the combatants pitted against each other the sum total of their physical endurance, national resources, and moral vigour. The scale was so large that it passed beyond the scope of any single directing mind or group of minds. Therefore its story cannot follow the neat model of earlier campaigns, but must be a tale of sound and fury, signifying much indeed, but without pattern or logic, for millions of men blundered blindly towards a decision.

Three things must be noted at the start. The problem before the world prior to 1914 was how to use its new mastery of nature to maximise human life. Needing peace for constructive work more than any preceding age, it was swept suddenly into a barbarous struggle for mere existence. The General Staffs might have their plans, but the peoples were in confusion. Again, the State in recent years had become a more potent thing, and the dogmas of a dozen schools of political thought had exalted its authority ; men looked to it to provide a new way of life, and, having acknowledged this sovereignty, they submitted when they were offered a new way of death. It was a war of nations, and of docile nations. Lastly, it was a struggle which enlisted the enthusiasm of a youth long puzzled and uneasy. The legend that young men were sacrificed by bellicose dotards is childishly false. The elderly laboured for peace and faced the inevitable with heavy hearts. But in every belligerent capital youth clamoured for war.

Mr. Asquith, when on August 6th he moved the Vote of Credit, laid down the purpose of Britain as the fulfilment of a solemn international obligation and the vindication of law against lawless force. For this task, which the nation accepted with few dissidents, what assets could we furnish? Our Army was meagre as compared with those of our allies and opponents. Britain had deliberately chosen to limit herself to a small highly trained force, trusting to the protection of her Navy to allow her to improvise an adequate Army in the event of a great war : she had followed Raleigh's precept—" There is a certain proportion both by sea and land beyond which excess brings nothing but disorder and amazement." · She had reserved her strength for a long sustenance of effort ; as Germany hoped for immediate victory, so Britain thought of the ultimate battle. Her resources, provided the issue were not decided in the early months, would steadily grow, for, unlike her neighbours, she had but skimmed the cream of her man power for the first trial and had not depleted her wealth by extravagant armaments.

But for immediate use she had only her Expeditionary Force, which numbered 160,000 troops of all arms. Small as this striking force was, it was not to be compared with any continental army of the same size. The British regulars were beyond question the most professional in the world. A large proportion of both men and officers had had actual experience of war, and a man who has already led or followed successfully under fire has learned something that no textbook or staff college or manœuvres can teach. In Carnot's famous words: " It is not pirouetting up and down a barrack-yard, but active service that makes an old soldier." Behind it lay the Territorial Force, not yet brought up to strength and still imperfectly trained, and behind that the civilian manhood of the country, now flocking to every recruiting station.

Britain was not, like certain continental states, a nation in arms, but she had exceptional facilities for becoming a nation at war. She had in her industrial machine an almost unlimited means of producing war material, she had great wealth, and she had a world-wide network of commerce. The use of these advantages and the feeding of her people depended on keeping her naval predominance unimpaired. She had never been stronger afloat than when at 8.30 on the morning of August 4th her Grand Fleet put to sea. Her naval strength was far greater than that of Germany and Austria combined ; she had been a pioneer in every modern invention, and in every class of craft she had a superiority both in numbers and quality. In two respects only was the Navy at a disadvantage as compared with the Army. Modern warfare for it was still an untested thing. Scarcely an admiral had had any experience of actual sea-fighting. We had to prove in practice a new technique under conditions which we could forecast but which we did not know. Again, on our Navy depended utterly our hope not of victory alone but of national survival. Expeditionary force after expeditionary force might be beaten and disappear, but they could be replaced ; but a decisive defeat at sea would mean the end of Britain and the downfall of her allies. In Mr. Churchill's words, the Commander-in-Chief of the British Grand Fleet was the only man who could lose the war in an afternoon.

So with a small expert Army, capable of indefinite expansion, and a Navy omnipotent by all reasonable presumptions, we entered upon a war of a type wholly novel in our history. Hitherto in the great European struggles we had subsidised continental allies, had controlled the seas, and, using our sea power, had flung in small armies at vital points. Now we had to take our place in the forefront of the main theatre. There was no commander anywhere who had been trained to war on the grand scale ; the continental staffs had worked out grandiose schemes, but their solutions were only academic ; it was realised that most of the problems would be different from those of the past.

But all the world failed in exact prevision, and in the necessary guessing guessed wrong. It was universally assumed, for example, that the coming war would be one of movement and manœuvre. It was believed, too, that modern numbers and weapons would make the struggle most desperate but also short, since flesh and blood would soon be brought to the breaking point. No belligerent recognised the immense increase of strength given by modern weapons to the defence over the attack, and the consequent impregnability of field entrenchments.

CONTACT

Again, none foresaw the vital problem of the superior direction of the whole Allied strength, the need of finding some controlling mind which was capable of disregarding all but the simple essentials and taking the broad synoptic view. Men looked for too little from the new factors in war, and they looked for too much. In many ways the world was blind to the meaning of its own progress, but in other respects it was too ready to assume that the former things, the eternal truths of strategy, had passed away.

That such problems did not trouble the mind of statesmen more acutely at the start was due to the fact that the contest was regarded as likely to be brief. The thing would be like the clashing of two great forces of nature, and the human mind must be content in large measure to wait upon fortune. No man foresaw that presently the whole strength of every belligerent would be involved, that scarcely a corner of the globe would be free from turmoil, and that the supreme need on each side would be some central direction, political, moral and military, such as in the Seven Years' War the elder Pitt gave to his country.

Britain was fortunate in having at the outset one great combatant figure on which the popular mind could lean. Lord Kitchener was stopped at Dover as he was leaving for Egypt, and on August 6th became Secretary of State for War. It was a wise appointment, for the public had created an image of him to suit its fancy, and that image, false as it was in many points, was well calculated to win confidence. He was no politician, and Britain was surfeited with politics. He had that air of mystery and taciturnity which the ordinary man loves to associate with a great soldier. His splendid presence, his iron face, his glittering record, raised him out of the ranks of mere notabilities to the elect circle of those who even in their lifetime become heroes of romance. As it happened, the popular judgment, though right in spirit, was wrong on most of the facts. Lord Kitchener had little gift for detail and he was a poor administrator. He was fond of summary methods, and the result was often confusion. He was not a comfortable member of a team. So far from being a man of iron and granite, he was often lonely and conscious of it, often undecided, too loyal sometimes to be wise, and too tender-hearted to be just. His underrating of the Territorials was to be a grave hindrance to the British effort. But he had the invaluable gifts of foresight and imagination, though to his long-sighted eyes the foreground might sometimes be dim. He did not foresee trench warfare and was perplexed when it began, but his instinct told him that the war would be lengthy and he made his preparations accordingly. In Mr. Lloyd George's apt image, he illuminated by flashes and not by a steady glow, " like one of those revolving lighthouses which radiate momentary gleams of revealing light far into the surrounding gloom, and then suddenly relapse into complete darkness."

The one war plan which mattered at the start was Germany's, as laid down by Schlieffen. This was to hold Russia with small forces, and direct the main weight of her strength to a surprise encirclement of France on the north. If France attempted an attack on her weak left wing by way of Lorraine, so much the better, for the thing, as Captain Liddell Hart has put it, would be like a revolving door—if a man

pressed heavily on one side the other side would
swing round and hit him in the back.   France, under
the influence of the mysticism of the *offensive à outrance*,
under-estimated the strength of the German right
wing and the width of its sweep, and her ill-fated
Plan XVII aimed at meeting it by a counter-attack
on the enemy centre and left.   The French intelligence system was faulty, and the campaign opened
with the British Expeditionary Force—in spite of the
doubts of Kitchener and French and Haig—stuck
on as an appendix to the French left in what was
to prove the most perilous part of the battle-field.
Germany not without reason hoped for an early and
crushing victory, a " battle without a morrow "
before the leaves fell.   France, with less reason, put
blind trust in her historic prowess in war and in the
proven valour of her sons.   Britain launched her
little army into the void with the anxiety with which
men and nations face something which is new in
their experience but on which hang mighty issues.

> Far other is this battle in the west,
> Whereto we move, than when we strove in youth
> And brake the petty kings.

II

In this place we are not concerned with a detailed
history of the War, but only with its main tidal movements, as seen from the view-point which is given
by the lapse of two decades.

Germany in the first stage had the odds on her side.
She was superior to any combination of her enemies
in the number of trained men she could put straight-
way into the field ; she had a smooth and powerful

military machine, built up patiently during a generation ; she had a centralised command and a colleague
subject in all matters to her will. She was aware
that her opponents had greater potential strength, but
it would take time to become actual, and long before
that day dawned she hoped for victory. She came
near succeeding. The Belgian defence scarcely
delayed her time-table. France's counter-move in
the south failed bloodily, and her dislocated armies,
ill-placed along a wide frontier, were faced with
the ruin of all their elaborate plans and a deadly
menace from the north. The French left just escaped
in time from the net, and the British army, in a predica-
ment still more hazardous, was compelled like its
neighbour to a retreat which was not strategic but
enforced and blind.

Nevertheless two delaying actions, at Le Cateau
by the British and at Guise by the French, upset
in turn Germany's calculations. Her right, instead
of encircling and taking Paris, wheeled inward to
attempt a second Sedan. Schlieffen's plan was
abandoned, and while the speed of the advance
slackened from fatigue and failure of supplies, a new
envelopment was attempted on her left and left
centre by way of Nancy and Verdun. Joffre, the
French Commander-in-Chief, divined this fumbling
in the German High Command, reshuffled his forces,
and revised his earlier plans. In the first days of
September a flank attack, of which Gallièni, the
Governor of Paris, was the inspirer, so embarrassed
the German right that a thirty-mile gap was created
between the armies of Kluck and Bülow. Verdun
and Nancy stood firm against the assault on the other
flank ; the British force, turning at long last, marched

into the gap on Bülow's right ; on September 9th Bülow began to fall back, and by the 11th the whole German army was in retreat.

Such were the elements of the First Battle of the Marne, which to the British people, disheartened by the *débâcle* in the north and straining their eyes anxiously into the mist, came as a miracle and a mystery. The Allies had snatched a strategic victory from the enemy's blunders. The central guidance on Germany's side had gone to pieces, and Moltke in consequence disappeared. Germany failed, as Marmont failed at Salamanca, because she allowed a perilous crack to open in her front, a crack due to the defects in her whole strategy of envelopment. That strategy demanded the impossible, and placed a burden of co-ordination and control upon her High Command which it could not sustain. The First Marne was a relic of the old regime of war, a battle of movement, surprise, improvisation—which is to say that it was won less by the machine than by the human quality of the soldier. Joffre, surmounting his earlier delusions, managed tardily to seize the strategic initiative, aided by the inspired audacity of Gallièni and the stubborn defence of Foch and Sarrail and Castelnau. It was the most significant battle of the War—decisive, inasmuch as it shattered the first German plan of campaign. The " battle without a morrow " had gone beyond hope, for the battle had been fought and the morrow had come.

But in another sense it was not decisive ; it did not, like Jena, destroy one of the combatant forces, or make peace inevitable, like Sadowa and Solferino. Germany kept her armies in being, and made a skilful retreat in the face of an unskilful pursuit. By

September 13th she had re-knit her front on the north
bank of the Aisne, and established the first battlements
of that fortress which she was to hold for four years.
But she was not yet on the defensive. The plan of
Falkenhayn, who had succeeded Moltke, was to
envelop the Allied left flank, and secure those Channel
ports which might have fallen to Germany as easy
fruit during the Allied retreat in August—a peril
which would have crippled the British effort and to
which only Mr. Churchill seemed awake. The
Allies retorted with attempts to turn their enemy's
right flank, and the campaign took the form of a race
to the sea.

Germany's first business was to get rid of the
Belgian Army, based on the fortified camp of Antwerp.
Her powerful artillery blasted a hole in the defence,
the Belgian field force withdrew to the Flanders coast
covered by the newly arrived British 7th Division,
and, though the garrison was strengthened on Mr.
Churchill's initiative by three British brigades of
marines and naval volunteers, the city was forced to
surrender on October 10th. Its resistance had not
been in vain, for it had delayed the main German
outflanking movement long enough to enable the
Allies to fill the seaward gap. For a fortnight the
latter believed that they were engaged in a promising
offensive, and optimism reigned in the minds of both
French and British commanders, who speculated
pleasantly on what date they were likely to cross the
enemy frontier. But by October 20th they began to
realise that their task would be a desperate effort to
hold their ground, for Falkenhayn, bringing troops
from his left and centre and using his new formations,
was staking everything on a break through to the

west and an outflanking which he believed might be decisive.

So began the First Battle of Ypres, on the rim of upland east of the old Flemish city. In the north the Belgian Army held its ground in the mud of the Yser, having opened the sluices and flooded the plain ; on the south the Messines ridge was lost after heavy fighting ; but in the centre, in the half-moon of the Ypres salient, the troops of Britain and France for a fortnight beat off the attack in a string of confused and costly actions. There was no general plan and no central leading. Foch and French rarely understood what was happening and contributed little beyond an ill-founded optimism ; the brunt fell upon Haig, his divisional and brigade commanders, and above all on the regimental officers. There were moments, as on October 29th, 30th and 31st, and November 11th, when only a miracle seemed to save our thin front from destruction. It was, like Albuera, a soldiers' battle, won by the dogged fighting quality of the rank-and-file rather than by any tactical brilliance ; there was no room and no time for ingenious tactics. Much of it was a wild mellay in which units became hopelessly mixed and strange things happened. A subaltern often found himself in command of a battalion ; a brigadier commanded one or two companies, or a division, as the fates ordained. The price paid was high. On the British side whole units virtually disappeared. One divisional general, ten brigadiers, nearly a dozen staff officers fell, and eighteen regiments and battalions lost their colonels. Scarcely a house famous in our stormy history but mourned a son. Wellesley, Wyndham, Dawnay, FitzClarence, Cadogan, Cavendish,

Bruce, Gordon-Lennox, Fraser, Kinnaird, Hay, Hamilton—it was like the death-roll after Agincourt or Flodden. But it was a victory, for it achieved its purpose. The Allied line stood firm from the Oise to the sea, and the enemy's short-lived initiative was over.

On the Eastern Front the great spaces and the slower concentration of armies made the first stage of the campaign more tentative and diffused. Russia at once invaded East Prussia, which eased the situation in the west by drawing two German corps from the Marne. But when Hindenburg and Ludendorff succeeded the incompetent Prittwitz, the invasion came to a disastrous end in the annihilation of Samsonov at Tannenberg and the flight of Rennenkampff across the border. Meantime Austria had got herself into difficulties. Her invasion of Poland had been checked by the end of August, her right wing in Galicia was threatened, and by the close of September she was in general retreat. With the help of Germany a fresh attempt was made to advance to Warsaw, but it was checked by the movement of a group of Russian armies against Silesia. Hindenburg used his smaller forces to brilliant purpose, and retired, destroying the scanty Polish communications. Intercepting the enemy's uncoded wireless messages, he drove a wedge into the Russian front, forced one half back on Warsaw, and at Lodz decisively defeated the other. The end of the year saw the Russian armies stubbornly on the defensive on the river line west of the Polish capital.

Austria had a luckless autumn. She failed to clear Galicia, and relieve the beleaguered Przemysl, and the most she could do was to hold the enemy on the line of the Donajetz, and to block the Carpathian passes and the way to the Hungarian cornlands. She was no more fortunate in Serbia. Her first attack had been beaten off, and a later and more elaborate invasion was shattered in a great battle in the first week of December, when her army lost most of its guns and was reduced to a mob of fugitives. Midwinter, which on the Eastern Front meant a certain lull in the fighting, found Austria, with a record of misfortune behind her, on the defensive less than forty miles from Cracow, and Russia, after checks, defeats and confusions, in a like attitude about the same distance from Warsaw. The honours were with Germany.

At sea there had been no surprises. Till the defences of Scapa Flow were ready the Grand Fleet led a dangerous nomadic life among Scottish inlets. But from the first day of war the British Navy had its stranglehold upon Germany, to whom only the Baltic was left of the waters of the globe. Opportunities were missed, as when the German cruisers *Goeben* and *Breslau* were suffered to escape, and thereby Turkey's hostility was assured, and at the start there was some fumbling on minor points which led to losses, but in all the greater matters its competence was supreme. The Expeditionary Force crossed to France unhindered. On August 29th our battle-cruisers and destroyer flotillas successfully raided the Bight of Heligoland. German warships on foreign duty were hunted down, and Von Spee's success at Coronel was avenged by his destruction on December 8th at the Falkland Islands. Our sea-power enabled us to gather in the German colonies, and to dispose of German merchantmen on the high seas.

Sir John Jellicoe, realising that the British Navy was the main buttress of the Allied armies, was ready for battle, but was resolved not to imperil the future by unwisely seeking it, since without a battle he was able to reap most of the fruits of victory. The cautious Fabian in the north had now his corrective and complement at the Admiralty, for at the close of October Lord Fisher became again First Sea Lord. Explosive, erratic, a dangerous enemy, a difficult friend, this " proud and rebellious creature of God " had the breadth of imagination and the sudden lightning flashes of insight which deserve the name of genius. Behind a smoke screen of rhodomontade, his powerful mind worked on the data of a vast experience. His policy in war might be too bold or too whimsical, but it would never be timorous or supine.

III

Had some celestial intelligence, such as Mr. Hardy has presented in *The Dynasts*, kept an eye on the campaign—an intelligence with a vision unhindered by time or by space—he would have had certain comments to make at the close of the year 1914. He would have observed the War quickly extending its area. Its periphery was still in flux, but in the centre, which was the Western Front, the dynamic was fast hardening into the static. Britain, he might have commented, was being drawn into a mode of war which was a new thing in her history, and which was alien to all her former principles. Her alliance

with France had bound her for the moment to a
military creed which was not her own, and which was
based on the mysticism of Clausewitz and a popular
misinterpretation of Napoleon. In the past she had
for the most part fought with a wary business eye,
and her mind had not been bemused with notions of
an " absolute " war, which her great captains like
Cromwell and Marlborough would have rejected
with scorn. She had never believed in battles for
their own sake, but had endeavoured to fight only
when she could fight at a profit. She had used her
command of the sea, her industrial power, her wealth
and her geographical position to wise strategic
purpose. But now she was in danger of nullifying
her traditional assets by letting herself be interlocked
in a land struggle of brute force, engaging the enemy
at his strongest instead of at his weakest point, and
without far-sighted purpose. She, the freest of all
the belligerents, was drifting into bondage to a false
theory and an out-moded machine. Would she
liberate herself before it was too late ?

The commentator would have admitted that
Germany's torrential invasion of France made it
necessary for a British force at once to cross the
Channel, but, remembering the effect on the enemy
mind of a single brigade of marines at Ostend, and
of the resistance of Antwerp, he would have reflected
that the view of French and Haig was perhaps right,
and that its proper place was on the Belgian coast on
the flank of the invader. He would have had only
praise for the conduct of the retreat from Mons,
when the British force was left in the dark by its
allies and pitchforked headlong into a novel and
intricate campaign. But he would have been critical

of many details of its turn at the Marne, since a more resolute advance should have brought it to the river by the night of September 8th ; of the too leisurely assault on the Aisne position, which might well have been pierced on the 13th ; above all, of the failure to send across the Channel some of our Territorial divisions and mounted brigades, which before and during the race to the sea might have worked havoc with the German communications. There was no controlling mind on the British side which was capable of the larger strategical purpose, a misfortune perhaps inevitable in the first stages of a new and unfamiliar mode of war.

The commentator would have had much to say of the fundamental errors of France and Germany—the folly of the former's initial plan : the departure of the latter from Schlieffen's careful provisions, a departure which nullified the advantage of her ruthlessness and made her sin to no purpose against international ethics. He would have found many points to criticise in Moltke's leadership, such as his withdrawal of two corps to the Eastern Front during the crisis of the Marne, and the lack of all proper control by Great Headquarters. He would have noted Falkenhayn's failure during First Ypres to follow Gröner's advice and transfer six corps to his right wing, a failure which cost him the battle ; and, while admitting the moral effect of the Allies' stand there, might have hinted that, if Haig had followed his first idea and withdrawn to the line of the canal, many thousands of British lives would have been saved in the coming years, and many futile offensives have been prevented.

But all wars are a tissue of blunders, and that side

wins which makes the fewest and the least material, and the commentator might have concluded that the ominous fact was not mistakes but the absence of positive artistry. It looked as if the minds of the combatants were sinking into a dull acceptance of the obvious, as if they were content to continue in the rut into which accidents of position and munition-ment had led them. So far there had only been two gleams of the higher intelligence—Galliéni's flank movement on Kluck, and the much-abused British expedition to Antwerp. The result was some-thing very like a deadlock on both land and sea.

IV

The first mood of the British people was enthusiasm and an uninformed confidence. This was presently succeeded by acute anxiety, as news came of the retreat from Mons, of the tumbling down of French and Belgian fortresses, of our little army astray in some unknown corner of France. The Marne gave us hope again, a hope scarcely impaired by rumours of the weakness of Russia, and the heavy death-roll of First Ypres was made endurable by a sense that our manhood had been gloriously tested. There was a rising tide of anger in the popular mind, as reports reached them of German barbarities and the hosts of Belgian fugitives gave the evidence of eyewitnesses. Ugly mob passions were awakened ; a mania for spy-hunting began ; the maker of the new British Army, Lord Haldane, fell into disrepute because of his former friendliness to Germany, and a great sailor, Prince Louis of Battenberg, was compelled to resign his post. But among plain folk there burned a very pure and simple fire of patriotism. The nation was wonderfully united. The Government had not to face the kind of attacks which Pitt suffered at the hands of Fox and his allies, and which in a lesser degree appeared in the South African War.

An opposition quickly formed, but it was small in numbers and intellectually inconsiderable. It contained the men who, whether from generosity or perversity of spirit, must always side with the minority. It was sufficient for such that Germany should be widely unpopular ; instantly they discovered merits in the German case. Others were so rooted in a stubborn British confidence that they could not conceive of any danger to their liberties, and, distrusting after the British fashion all politicians, convinced themselves that their country's interests were being sacrificed to some shoddy political game. Some out of a gross spiritual pride conceived that the ethical principle which brought the nation into war must needs be wrong, since it was so generally accepted. There were the few genuine pacifists to whom war on any ground was abhorrent ; there were various practitioners of minor arts and exponents of minor causes who resented anything which distracted attention from them and their works. But whether the cause was moral arrogance, or temperamental obstinacy, or vanity, or mere mental confusion, the anti-war party was negligible. The nation had never been so wholly at one.

But it was not yet completely awake. The ordinary Briton was indignant with Germany because of her doings in Belgium, because she seemed to him to be the author of the war, and because her creed violated all the doctrines in which he had been taught to

believe. He was determined to beat her and to draw
her fangs. But he had as yet no realisation of the
hideous actualities of modern battles, or of the
solemnity of the crisis for civilisation, for his country,
and for himself. It was still to him a professional
rather than a national war. The human mind is
slow to visualise the unknown, and the smoke of a
burning homestead is a more potent aid to vision
than the most graphic efforts of the war corre-
spondent or the orator. We were unfortunate, too,
in our handling of the press. Britain, with her free
traditions, made a bad censor, and in official secrecy
she went far beyond what was demanded by military
requirements. The people knew little of the doings
of their army, and regiments were rarely mentioned.
A civilian First Lord at the Admiralty, and a civilian
Home Secretary dealing with many military questions, involved as their logical corollary a large
measure of free public criticism. To withdraw this
right by withdrawing reasonable information was to
make of our constitution a bureaucracy without a
bureaucracy's efficiency.

In spite of these hindrances the system of voluntary
recruiting did not break down ; indeed it justified
itself beyond the hopes of its warmest advocates.
Britain could not call upon her youth to enlist, as
France could, for the defence of home and kin ; she
could only ask it to fight for her honour and interests
—great matters, no doubt, but appealing to a more
limited class than a call to resist direct invasion. Yet
in the mellow autumn weather every training-camp
was crowded, and the English roads echoed to the
tramp of hundreds of thousands of stalwart lads,
singing ribald songs to hymn tunes. The wind was

blowing "which scatters young men through the world." First came the Territorials, honest fellows who in apathetic years with small encouragement had prepared themselves for their country's defence. After them followed the natural adventurers, those whom we call born soldiers, and the scallywags who sought nothing better. Next came the sober con-scientious men, like Cromwell's New Model, who had a cause to fight for. And then the wind blew louder, and thousands were gathered in who had never dreamed at the start that the call was for them, but who were moved by those queer unrealised impulses which are deeper than thought. By Christmas fully two millions of the inhabitants of the British Isles were under arms, either for home defence or foreign service.

The British recruitment was aided by the superb response of the British Empire. Germany had always despised this loose friendly aggregation, believing that the first whiff of grape-shot would shatter it, for to Germany Empire meant a machine, where each part was under the exact control of a central power. But the British conception was the reverse of mechanical. She had created a spiritual bond—

> Which, softness' self, is yet the stuff
> To hold fast where a steel chain snaps.

By her gift of liberty she had made the conquered her allies, and the very men she had fought became in her extremity her passionate defenders.

The muster of the Empire was a landmark in British history, greater perhaps than the War which was its cause. No man can read without emotion the tale of those early days in August when from every corner of the globe poured in appeals for the right to share in our struggle. Would that we had had a Homer to write a new Catalogue of the Ships! The free Dominions offered all their resources. In South Africa, Louis Botha, the ablest of our recent opponents in the field, became a British general. No unit, however small or remote, was backward in this noble emulation. India, whose alleged disloyalty had been a prime factor in German calculations, rose in every quarter and class to the supreme heights of sacrifice.

Small wonder that the news stimulated recruiting in Britain, for there was a sense of a vast new comradeship which stirred the least emotional. This rally of the Empire brought under one banner the trapper of Athabasca, the stockman from Victoria, the Dutch farmer from the back-veld, the tribesman of the Khyber, the gillie from the Scottish hills, and the youth from the London back streets. Racially it united Mongol and Aryan, Teuton and Celt; politically it drew to the side of the Canadian democrat the Indian feudatory whose land was still mediæval; spiritually it joined Christianity in all its forms with the creeds of Islam, Buddha, Brahma, and a thousand little unknown gods. The British commonwealth had revealed itself as that wonderful thing for which its makers had striven—a union based not upon statute and officialdom, but upon the eternal simplicities of the human spirit. In 1909 Lord Morley had taken as a *reductio ad absurdum* of the dream of Empire the notion that Australia would ever consent to pay for a war undertaken on behalf of Belgian neutrality. Yet now Australian troops were on the sea to give their lives in that cause.

V

To the King, as to his subjects, the outbreak of war meant the quieting of old feuds and an end to the threatened constitutional impasse. But, as to his subjects, only in a higher degree, it brought new and crushing anxieties. He saw men closely akin to him by blood the subject of popular odium and in the forefront of the nation's enemies. The people in the crisis had turned instinctively to him, and their deep and universal trust increased the burden of his responsibilities. Unlike his Ministers in council and his soldiers in the field, he had no plain task which could absorb his energies. His duty was only to wait and watch, while the old fabric of Europe was crumbling. The words which he had spoken the month before his Coronation must have often recurred to his mind. The " treasures of the past " were in jeopardy, and dark indeed was " the path of the future."

On the last day of November he paid his first visit to the Front. He saw Sir John French at St. Omer, and the headquarters of every corps and division ; he inspected the base and field hospitals, and from the little hill of Scharpenberg looked over the battle-ground of Ypres. President Poincaré, M. Viviani and General Joffre joined him at St. Omer, and at Furnes he met the King of the Belgians. It was the first time that a King of England had visited a French battle-front where his troops fought in company with their ancient foe. A dramatic proof of the new alliance was that descendants of Napoleon's marshals, Ney and Murat, were attached to the British Staff.

CONTACT

That visit in the bleak December weather had a special significance, for at Ypres an older world had vanished. A fortnight earlier, within hearing of the enemy guns sounding their last challenge, had passed our most famous soldier. Lord Roberts had come to visit his beloved Indian troops, had fallen ill of pleurisy, and had died on the night of November 14th. It was fitting that the master-gunner should die within hearing of his guns, and that the most adored of British captains should breathe his last amid the troops he had loved so well. With him went the army which he had commanded and done much to create. First Ypres saw the apotheosis of the British regulars, but also their end. A large part of the old " Contemptibles " was dead, and what was left was soon to be distributed among a thousand new battalions.

But the memory of the type remains—perhaps the most wonderful fighting man that the world has seen. Officers and men were curiously alike. Behind all the differences of birth and education there was a common temperament ; a kind of humorous realism about life, a dislike of tall talk, a belief in inherited tradition and historic ritual, a rough-and-ready justice, a deep cheerfulness which was not inconsistent with a surface pessimism. They generally took a dark view of the immediate prospect ; therefore they were never seriously depressed. They had an unshakable confidence in the ultimate issue ; therefore they never thought it worth mentioning. They were always slightly puzzled ; therefore they could never be completely at a loss ; for the man who insists on having the next steps neatly outlined before he starts will be unnerved if he cannot see his way ; whereas

129

others will drive on cheerfully into the mist, because they have been there before, and know that on the further side there is clear sky.

It was the end of an old army, and an older and freer mode of war. For now a huge, cumbrous mechanism had cast a blight of paralysis on human endeavour. The fronts had been stricken by their vastness into stagnation. Already a man could walk by a chain of outposts from Switzerland to the Vosges, and in a ditch from the Vosges to the North Sea.

CHAPTER II

THE FORTRESS

I

AT the beginning of 1915 the sky for the Allies was overcast, but the clouds were not yet threatening. Japan had joined them, but her effort must be confined to the Far East ; Italy was moving to their side ; Turkey had declared for Germany, while Bulgaria, Greece and Rumania were uneasy neutrals. Politically there was no cause for disquiet ; but on the battle-field there was an ugly jam. In the East the steam-roller of Russia seemed inclined, if anything, to roll backwards, and in the West the Allies found themselves set down before a bristling fortress. The front there could not be turned, since there were no flanks ; the only methods that appeared possible were investment and direct assault, and the first was slow and the second costly.

To the French command this prospect was not discouraging. They believed that the War could be won only on the front which was on French or Belgian soil, and that steady attack—*la guerre d'usure*—would presently wear down resistance. Such a plan, since surprise was impossible, could only succeed by so great an accumulation of munitions and men as would by brute force blast a way through. It underrated the enemy's material strength and the stubbornness of his spirit. This unimaginative loyalty to the commonplace was to cripple the Allied strategy at the moment when it had the chance of a free field, and before its blunders had made escape impossible.

To Britain it fell to make an effort to break this bondage, and, because she made it half-heartedly, to fail. The Western Front was clearly the *main* theatre of war, but was it necessarily the *decisive* theatre ? Might not an effort elsewhere so weaken Germany that defeat in the West would become inevitable ? The British Government early in January, having received an urgent appeal for help from Russia, began to ask themselves questions. Was there nothing to be said for the traditional British strategy of using our naval power to apply military force at unexpected points ? Was there not a danger that Joffre's policy of attrition might be so slow as to entail the bankruptcy of the conqueror ? We were confronted in Europe with a veritable fortress, but, if the principal gates were strongly held, were there no unguarded back-doors ? A great scheme-making began among Ministers and their technical advisers. Lord Fisher favoured a descent on the Schleswig-Holstein coast ; Mr. Lloyd George's fancy dwelt first on Salonika ; but in the end the plan which won unanimous support was Mr. Churchill's for the clearing of the Dardanelles and the taking of Constantinople. Success there would give immense and perhaps decisive results, for it would open the way for supplies to Russia, would bring in Italy and the wavering Balkan Powers on the Allied side, would put Turkey out of the war, and would make possible a deadly flank assault against Austria, Germany's ally.

THE FORTRESS

In the words of the official historian of the enterprise, the Western Front was a gamble with pounds for a gain of pence, the Dardanelles scheme a good chance of pounds for a stake of pennies. For the wager at the first was small. It was proposed to make the attack by sea alone, and to use in it some of our older battleships, destined presently for the scrapheap. There were obvious dangers, and the weight of historical authority was against the success of ships' guns against land forts, but it was fair to argue that the advance in naval gunnery and the use of aeroplanes for spotting had changed the situation.

What followed is a tragic example of an opportunity missed, and of a great enterprise nullified by a failure of nerve. On March 18th the attack on the Straits was launched. Most of the forts were silenced, and the thing seemed to be proceeding well until suddenly three battleships were lost from drifting mines. The action was broken off, and Admiral de Robeck declined to renew it until an army was ready to support him. Turkey at her last gasp was to her amazement given a breathing-space, of which she made brilliant use. Her resistance that day was the last effort of which she was at the moment capable, for she was almost destitute of munitions. Her Government had its papers packed, and was ready to leave for the uplands of Asia Minor. It was the drifting mines which decided our naval staff, and their presence was a fantastic accident. Ten days before a little Turkish steamer, the *Nousret*, had eluded the British night patrol of destroyers and laid a new line of twenty mines in Eren Kui Bay. On March 16th some of these mines were found and destroyed by our sweepers, but we did not realise that they were part of a line of mines, and so we did not look for more. Had we made a different deduction there would have been no casualties on the 18th, and de Robeck on the 19th or 20th would have taken his fleet into the Sea of Marmora. The officer in charge of the little *Nousret* probably never knew of the fatefulness of a deed which altered the whole course of the War.

Britain was now committed to a joint expedition, for it appeared that there were troops available for an attack by land. But success depended upon the provision of adequate forces, and that again depended upon a temporary defensive on the Western Front and a refraining from expensive assaults. Lord Kitchener unhappily halted between two opinions. He chose to fight at Gallipoli with only the loose fringe of Britain's military strength, which was patently insufficient even for a first blow, and reinforcements for which could only be wrung from the West in the face of bitter opposition. It was the old story of the Sibylline books. We purchased failure in the end at a price which a month or two before would have assured triumphant success. Mr. Churchill's summary is the bare truth :

Three divisions in February could have occupied the Gallipoli peninsula with little fighting ; five could have captured it after March 18th ; seven were insufficient by the end of April, but nine might just have done it. Eleven might have sufficed at the beginning of July. Fourteen were to prove insufficient on August 7th.

The story of the Dardanelles is one of the noblest and cruellest in the War. Had it been possible for the Allies to forgo their futile offensives in the West in 1915, for which they were not ready, to hold the line there to the stalemate which Germany's pre-occupation in Russia would not have permitted her to break, and to concentrate on cutting their way through to Constantinople, they would have succeeded, and the final battle on the Western Front would have been antedated by months, perhaps by years. But such prevision is for the immortals and not for fallible men ; and in the spring of 1915 there seemed to be cogent reasons for the wrong conclusion. The tale of the campaign is one of superb feats of arms, from the landing on April 25th to the final August failure at Suvla, when fine troops were squandered by old and feeble generals. Of the commander-in-chief, Sir Ian Hamilton, it may fairly be said that he made few mistakes, and that he showed a resource and a resolution which were only too rare in British leadership. *Si Pergama dextra defendi possent etiam hac defensa fuissent.* The expedition closed with a miracle, when at the end of the year the peninsula was evacuated, in defiance of all precedent, without a casualty. The European shore of the Narrows had now become not less famous than the opposite coast and the plain of Troy. Had the fashion endured of linking the strife of men with the gods, what strange myth would not have sprung from this rescue of British troops in the teeth of winter gales and uncertain seas ! It would have been rumoured, as at Troy, that Poseidon had done battle for his children.

II

On the Western Front 1915 was a year of dupes. France, passionately eager to recover her lost territory, fell into a strategic coma, with the consequence that her armies and those of Britain were hurled idly against a fortress-wall and broken. We believed that each assault weakened the enemy's resisting power, and by a fantastic arithmetic convinced ourselves that his losses were out of all proportion to our own, when the truth was that the attrition fell on the attack rather than on the defence.

The strength of the German fortifications was now recognised, and a theory of the offensive was developed. If a sufficiently powerful artillery fire was accumulated upon a section of the front, parapets and wire entanglements could be blown to pieces, and if the artillery, lengthening its range, were able to put a barrage between the enemy and his supports, then infantry might advance in comparative safety. The difficulty came with the next step. The British attack at Neuve Chapelle in March, and the attempts at Festubert and in the Artois in the early summer, failed because of the narrowness of the front of assault. To tear a rent no more than five miles wide meant that time was given for local reserves to come up and hold the gap, so that the enemy's front hardened like concrete before the advance.

In April the Germans introduced a new weapon by their use of poison gas in the action known as the Second Battle of Ypres, but, having inadequate reserves, they were unable to exploit their success. The innovation was in defiance of the etiquette of civilised war, but it was no more inhumane than shells and bayonets and liquid fire. One consequence of this action, in which Britain suffered especially, was to draw popular attention to our weakness in munitions, and to inaugurate a strenuous campaign for increased production. In September Joffre gathered his strength for a great effort on each side of the wide salient now formed by the German lines in France. The assault was to be in Champagne and in the Artois, delivered on broad fronts, and preceded by a sustained and intensive bombardment, which it was hoped would smooth the path for the infantry, but which at the same time gave ample notice to the enemy. The French advance conspicuously failed ; that of the British between Lens and La Bassée won at Loos a remarkable initial success, which could not be exploited because of the bungling of the British High Command and the supineness of the French on our right.

The chief lesson of Loos was the need for still more artillery power, a lesson readily learned ; but there was a further moral which was only drawn by the discerning few—that, even with a wide front of attack, in a frontal assault of which the enemy was forewarned, wearied troops would be met by fresh reserves, and the battle would become stereotyped and end in stalemate. There was another omen, too, to which all were blind. In the first hours of Loos a Highland brigade advanced four miles, and passed beyond all but the last German trench line. Behind them there was no tactical plan, and no certainty of support, and their feat was set down as a noble madness. Nevertheless that madness contained the seeds of future success, for it had in it the rudiments of " infiltration "—the tactics by which storm-troops found weak places in a front and filtered through. Three years later, when we had learned what the enemy could teach us, the same method was applied by a master hand to break in turn each of the German defences.

Sir John French's conduct of Loos made his position impossible, and before the end of the year he was relieved of his command. He had many of the best qualities of the British soldier : he was humane, kindly, in close touch with his men ; but he was too old and too set in his ways for this type of war. He had himself little to contribute in the way of ideas, and his mind was shut to those of other people. He fought confusedly and gallantly by a plan which was not of his making, and which he often imperfectly understood. Haig, his successor, was of a different stamp. With greater steadfastness of character, he had far higher powers of mind. He, too, had prepossessions to get rid of, and, for one of his dogged, precise and conservative temperament, the process was slow. On this point alone he can be fairly criticised. There is a close parallel with Foch. The Frenchman was at the start too hasty and high-flying, the Scot too rigid and deliberate. When disaster and disappointment had sobered the one and quickened and clarified the mind of the other, they became great soldiers.

On the Eastern Front the year began with brighter promise for Russia. The winter battles in Masuria had indeed driven her back to the Niemen, but she had still her hold on Galicia, where in March she captured Przemysl, and she still menaced the Carpathian passes. Austria, foreseeing that Italy would soon take the field against her, threatened to make a separate peace unless her ally came to her rescue. Hindenburg and Ludendorff pressed her case, and Falkenhayn, who was contemplating a great attack upon the British right in France, unwillingly consented to use in the East his fresh reserves. It was a momentous decision, for a German attack upon the ill-munitioned British Army, before its new troops were ready, might have decided the war. The German generals in the East, and the Austrian Conrad, believed that by a great effort Russia could be finally put out of action. Falkenhayn differed ; she could be crippled, he thought, but no more ; and he would consent only to a limited operation, which if necessary could be broken off to permit of a transfer of troops to the West.

Yet the attack which opened on May 2nd on the line of the Donajetz was so brilliantly directed and so overwhelmingly successful that at first it seemed as if Hindenburg's dream had come true. It was led by Mackensen, a master of speed and surprise, and his chief of staff was Seeckt, who after the war was to rebuild the German Army. Tactically it was the forerunner of the method of infiltration. Although outnumbered by nearly half a million, Mackensen in three days was in open country, and in a fortnight had advanced ninety-five miles. By the end of May the Russians were behind the San and the Dniester. In June Lemberg was retaken, and there was no enemy left in Galicia. The task was now to cut off the Warsaw salient, and on August 4th Warsaw fell. But Russia was now retreating on better communications, and, though Kovno and Brest Litovsk and Vilna were abandoned, by the autumn she had found a line on which she could stand. For Germany it was a conspicuous triumph in the field, and she now had Poland in her hands. But her enemy was unconquered, for Russia had retreated into those wastes of wood and water which

139

had baffled Napoleon. . . . She was presently to retreat into more impenetrable wastes of the spirit.

On the rout of Russia there followed the over-running of Serbia. Bulgaria, at last convinced of where her interests lay, threw in her lot with Germany, and in October German, Austrian and Bulgarian armies, under the direction of Mackensen, advanced against the little country from north and east. The Allies could give no effective aid, though weak British and French forces had landed at Salonika. The Serbs, a race of natural warriors who had few superiors, were driven in retreat through the Albanian mountains, and scarcely 100,000 soldiers reached the coast. British and Italian ships carried them to Corfu, where the remnant was rested and refitted and next year joined the Allies at Salonika. With the retreat went the aged King Peter, in whose strange soul burned the stubborn courage of his people. " I have struggled a great deal in my life," he said, " and I am tired, bruised and broken. But I shall not die before I see the victory of my country."

The year closed for Britain in shadows. Nowhere on the globe had the Allies improved their position. The various battles in the West had won little and cost much. Russia had retreated almost off the fighting map. Serbia had disappeared. Italy had entered the alliance, but was making little progress on her difficult fronts. The Gallipoli expedition had failed conspicuously, and had only been saved by a miracle from destruction. Our army in Mesopotamia, having attempted a vain dash for Bagdad, were now beleaguered in Kut. Our troops at Salonika were holding on grimly to a narrow littoral.

THE FORTRESS

The German submarine menace was daily growing, and the liner *Lusitania* and many merchant vessels had been sunk. German aircraft were bombing our coasts from the Thames to the Tyne, and official secrecy increased the rumours of our casualties. The honours of the year lay clearly with the enemy.

The inevitable result was criticism, the angry and often unjust criticism of a confused people. Hatred of the enemy was growing, fed by true and false tales of atrocities, and, since Britain is always a poor hater, the new mood made her acutely uncomfortable. The purpose of the nation was beyond question, but it was not being told what to do in order to achieve it. Men clutched at any proposal for organisation and discipline. Drink was the enemy, said Mr. Lloyd George, and the consequence was a dispute in which all sense of proportion was lost. In the end a compromise was reached under which Government control was established in scheduled areas, and the King set the example of voluntary abnegation by ordering that during the War no intoxicants should be served in the royal household. The country, it was widely felt, was not yet organised for war, and the questions of man-power for the armies and labour for the factories began to trouble the public mind. But first, as is the British habit, the critical blast fell on the civilian Government.

The fighting in the spring had made acute the business of munitions. The War Office was blamed for the shortage, though the blame was post-dated, for the improvement in the situation in September was to the War Office's credit. A Munitions Committee was formed in April, and a Ministry of Munitions in June, with Mr. Lloyd George as the presiding genius. He had found in the conduct of the War a cause which absorbed that energy which had once been given to domestic reform. A change in the Government was naturally demanded, and at the close of May the old Liberal Ministry was replaced by a coalition, which brought into the Cabinet Conservatives like Mr. Balfour, Lord Curzon, Lord Lansdowne, Mr. Austen Chamberlain and Mr. Bonar Law, and a representative of Labour in Mr. Arthur Henderson. One grotesque result was that Mr. Churchill, who was like a panther among polar bears, was relegated to the lowest Cabinet post, and that Lord Haldane, the Army's creator, was left out altogether. The new Cabinet had no great merit beyond its novelty, for, though it was composed of able men, the machine was too cumbrous for swift and consistent action. The most hopeful fact was that in the work of the Munitions Ministry an attempt was at last made to enlist business talent in the public service. It was not till November that the mechanism was improved by the creation of a small strategic Cabinet of five—the Prime Minister himself, the Chancellor of the Exchequer, Mr. Balfour, Mr. Bonar Law and Mr. Lloyd George.

There was also heard for the first time criticism of our military leadership. Lord Kitchener had lost much of his earlier prestige, for he had had to bear the blame for all our failures. But there were profounder causes of disquiet. The nation was militarily too uninstructed to grasp the faults of our battle tactics in the West, but many were beginning to realise that, taking the War as a whole, we lacked any serious and consistent strategic plan. We had made adventures without counting the cost, we had drifted into impossible situations, and had suffered the enemy to dictate our line of policy. Reasonable men had come to believe that a reform of our military machine, and not a shuffling of Ministers, was the vital question. The first need was for a competent General Staff at home, for Lord Kitchener had been compelled to act as his own General Staff, and before the end of the year Sir William Robertson was brought back to the War Office. It was an improvement in our domestic mechanism, but it left untouched the more urgent question of a central command for all the Allies in the West.

But the two subjects which most agitated the popular mind were the temper of Labour and the matter of conscription. There had long been troubles on the Clyde, in South Wales and elsewhere, and the new munitions policy, with its wholesale suspension of trade union rules, increased the tension. Much foolish and unjust recrimination followed, which did not help matters, and till the end of the War, in spite of the high wages, industrial troubles were always on a hair-trigger. It was inevitable. There was a work-weariness as well as a war-weariness, factory-shock as well as shell-shock. British Labour reflected the mood of the country ; it had its moments of revolt and discontent as well as its steady hours of resolution. As the demand for an increase of the armies became more clamant it assumed a special importance. The first step was Lord Derby's attempt to organise recruiting on a more scientific basis. By the end of the year it was apparent that this organised voluntaryism had failed. The figures were published early in 1916, and after that it was only a matter of months till conscription followed.

There was small opposition in the country, and the attitude of organised Labour was one of the most characteristically British performances in the campaign. A Labour congress in January 1916, by a majority of a million card-votes, instructed the Labour Party in Parliament to oppose the measure. At the annual conference three weeks later the members approved of the War by a majority of nearly a million, rejected conscription by large majorities, by a small majority decided not to agitate for repeal should the measure become law, and by a very large majority agreed that the three Labour members should retain their posts in the Government. The result was a typical product of our national temperament, and only the thoughtless would label it inconsistent. The Labour delegates were honest men in a quandary. They were loath to give up a cherished creed even under the stress of a dire necessity. But they were practical men and Englishmen, and they recognised compelling facts. If they could not formally repudiate their dogmas, they could neglect them.

In the bewilderment of the year there was one incident which keyed the national temper to that point where resolution acquires the impetus of a passion. An Englishwoman, Miss Edith Cavell, the head of a nursing institute in Brussels, had been active in assisting the escape of wounded Allied soldiers. She was arrested, tried, and condemned, and on October 11th suffered death, in spite of the efforts of the American and Spanish Embassies to save her. Her execution was legal, since on the letter of the German military law she was liable to the extreme penalty, but in the case of a woman and a nurse, who had ministered to German sick and wounded,

the pedantry which exacted that penalty was an
outrage on human decency. In France and Britain,
in Holland and America, her execution woke a profound horror, for it seemed to reveal as by a flash-
light the psychology of that German " culture "
which sought to regenerate the world. So noble a
death should not be tarnished by facile praise. She
was not the least of that sisterhood of great-hearted
women who have taught the bravest men a lesson
in courage. M. Clemenceau spoke the tribute of the
people of France : " Since the day of Joan of Arc,
to whose memory I know that our Allies will one
day seek to erect a statue, England has owed us this
return. She has nobly given it."

The King since his accession had enjoyed remark-
ably good health ; indeed, save for his attack of
typhoid fever in 1898, he had never had a serious
illness. But on his visit to the front in October 1915
he met with an accident, carefully concealed from
the public, which might have had the gravest consequences. He landed at Boulogne and inspected the
base hospitals. Thence he travelled to Rouen and
Havre, and saw much of both the British and the
French work behind the lines. These visits were
strenuous affairs, for, apart from busy days filled
with long journeys, the King worked every morning
assiduously at the papers forwarded from London.
At Aire he found Sir Douglas Haig and reviewed
troops, and at Doullens he met President Poincaré,
who was splendidly attired in a blue yachting cap,
a blue cape coat, and yellow leggings. The next
halt was Amiens, where he was joined by General
Joffre, and there was a parade of four corps of the

Armée Coloniale. At Cassel he reviewed the British Second Army under General Plumer, and afterwards at Bailleul the Canadian Corps.

On Thursday, October 28th, came the accident. At Labuissière the King was received by Sir Douglas Haig, and reviewed the 4th Corps of Sir Henry Rawlinson and the 1st Corps of Sir Hubert Gough. He was proceeding to inspect a squadron of the Royal Flying Corps, when a sudden outbreak of cheering made his horse rear and fall back on him, slipping on the muddy ground. For a moment the King lay very still, and the onlookers feared the worst. But he struggled to his feet, and was carried to his car and taken back to Aire. So serious his accident seemed that the Prince of Wales left at once to report to the Queen. For two days the King remained in bed, but on November 1st he decided to return home. He was carried on a stretcher aboard the train and a hospital ship, and, after a rough crossing, reached Buckingham Palace in a motor ambulance at 8 p.m. He was well again in a day or two, but it was only by a narrow margin that Britain escaped what would have been the crowning mischance of a melancholy year.

III

When the year 1916 opened, the main front had been irrevocably fixed in the West. The vast material and mechanical power involved in the new type of war made it impossible to alter readily the type of campaign which had once been set, or to use the whole world-front to strategic purpose. The unimaginative methods of frontal attack and attrition,

146

as practised in 1915, were the only ones of which the High Command could conceive, since they seemed to follow naturally from the cumbrous mechanism behind them. The fact that they were costly was obscured by the hope that they were still more costly to the enemy. There was perhaps some reason in the view that the German will to conquer could only be broken by a holocaust of suffering, and not by some ingenious strategical triumph which might have given the Allies a victory on points, for we were fighting not only the pride of a monarch and an army but the megalomania of a great people.

The War had been thus stereotyped on a pattern, and the chief criticism must be that the pattern was not used to the best purpose. There was no unity of direction among the Allies in Western Europe, and a dreadful barrenness in tactical resource. As to the second, it may be said that the nature of the campaign was such as to atrophy tactical ingenuity ; as to the first, that no Allied Government at that stage could have proposed a unity of command, which would place its armies under a foreigner, without falling from power. Nor can much of the blame for the deadlock be laid on the British commanders. They had been compelled to conform to a mode of war which was not of their planning, and from which they could not now escape. The most that can be said is that, out of a kind of professional loyalty, they had been too ready to defend the indefensible. What could Haig have achieved had he protested against the whole system ? A radical change of military policy in the throes of a campaign would be like the uprooting of mandrakes.

Failing the appointment of a Generalissimo for the

whole front who had an eye for realities, the only hope of escape lay in the civilian Government of Britain, for that of France was bound to the chariot-wheels of her General Staff. Only British statesmen could break the bondage of a leaden and ineffective machine. If any charge is to be brought against them, it is not that they interfered unduly with the soldiers, but that they did not interfere enough, and in the right way. In a war of nations it is the civilian who must direct the general strategy, for, as Sir William Robertson has pointed out, in the total effort of a people in war only twenty-five per cent. is purely military. The French politician was right who said that war had become too grave a business to be left to the soldier. But the distinction between what is technical and professional, and therefore the soldier's special province, and what has a wider significance, is always hard to draw ; and at this stage there was no British statesman or British soldier who could see our work in the field in its true relation to the central purpose of the war.

The Chantilly Conference of December 1915 laid down the Allied plans for the coming year. There was to be a co-ordinated offensive on the Eastern, Western and Italian Fronts, and the minimum of effort elsewhere. Germany, aware of this scheme, resolved to forestall it. Falkenhayn regarded Russia as half paralysed and Italy as unimportant. The soul of the enemy attack was Britain, and she could only be reached through her ally France. Though outnumbered in the West by three to two, he would attack France at a point which she was bound to defend and at which her defence would bleed her to death. On February 20th 1916 his guns opened against Verdun, that border fortress whose fall in 1792 had drawn from Danton his famous " De l'audace, encore de l'audace, toujours de l'audace."

The defence of Verdun was France's greatest feat of arms in the campaign. She had much leeway to make up from past carelessness, but the peril steeled the spirit and steadied the nerve of the nation. First Pétain and then Nivelle, who in this task made his name, held the ground with a noble obstinacy. There were moments when all seemed over, but always there came some miraculous revival. For five desperate months the battle continued, and the recapture by the French of Thiaumont on the last day of June and the failure of the German attack at Souville on July 11th may be taken as the end of the main battle. Germany, believing like all the world in France's *élan* in attack, had misjudged her power of maintaining a long and desperate defence. As the weeks passed Verdun became for France a watch-word, a mystic symbol of her resolution. Mankind must have its shrines, and that thing for which much blood had been spilled becomes holy in its eyes. Over Verdun, as over Ypres, there will brood in history a strange aura, the effluence of the sacrifice and fortitude of the tens of thousands who fell before her gates. Her little hills are for ever consecrated by her dead.

The summer advances of Russia and Italy did something to relieve the pressure on Verdun, but the real distraction came on July 1st, when the main battle moved from the shattered Meuse uplands to the sluggish Somme and the green downs of Picardy. As the weary French infantry scrambled over the débris of Thiaumont, a hundred miles to the

north-west on a broad front the infantry of Britain
and France were waiting to cross their parapets. This
had been fixed at Chantilly as the main effort of the
year, but Verdun had seriously limited the French
divisions available. Haig would have preferred an
attack in Flanders, and indeed it is hard to see why
Joffre chose the Somme area, for the German position
there was immensely strong, and success offered no
strategic advantage.

The first day brought only slender results. There
was no chance of surprise, the lengthy bombardment,
owing to the poor quality of the ammunition, completely failed of its purpose, and the front of assault
was too wide and the pressure too uniform. We
were attacking a fortress without concentrating on
the weak spots. The battle, which continued till it
was stopped by the November rains, degenerated
into a colossal effort of attrition. The later phases
showed more tactical ingenuity than the earlier, and
they were made notable by the use—the premature
use—of a new weapon, the credit of which belonged
wholly to Britain. This was the Tank, which, after
more than a year of controversy and delay, was first
tried on September 15th. Its success did something
to convince the wiser minds in the British Command
that here had been found the method of overcoming
the defence of machine-guns, trenches and wire
entanglements which had hitherto paralysed the
attack.

The Somme was the first great effort of the new
armies of Britain, and in it they won much glory
and a grave. The " tawny ground of Picardy,"
which Shakespeare's Henry V discoloured with blood,
was to become memorable for the English people,

since few households in the land had not contributed
to it a son. It was the final witness of the entry
of the manhood of Britain into war. Most of the
troops engaged had twenty months before been
employed in peaceful civilian trades. In their ranks
were every class and condition—miners from the
north, factory hands from the industrial centres,
clerks and shop-boys, ploughmen and shepherds,
Saxon and Celt, college graduates and dock labourers,
men who in the wild places of the earth had often
faced danger, and men whose chief adventure had
been a Sunday bicycle ride. This fighting stuff, which
Germany had decried, proved a match for her
Guards and Brandenburgers.

It is not easy to judge fairly a battle of which the
guiding plan was so wasteful and uninspired. Yet
its results were vital, and the gains were on the whole
to the Allies. The losses on each side were approximately half a million—the Germans a little less, the
Allies a little more. The British armies were given
experience and were not discouraged : the Germans
lost notably in confidence, and their whole military
machine was put out of gear. Hindenburg and
Ludendorff, who had now replaced Falkenhayn,
found a very real decline in *moral* in the West. "The
German army," the latter wrote, "had been fought
to a standstill and was utterly worn out ; if the war
lasted, our defeat seemed inevitable." Britain had
lost in officers three times as much as her opponents,
but she had great resources to draw upon, and the
losses of Germany in this class could not be replaced.
The spirit both of her men in the field and of the
nation at large was gravely depressed. The Somme
became a name of terror, that " blood-bath " to

which many journeyed and from which few returned.
Of what avail her easy conquests on the Danube
when this deadly cancer in the West was eating
into her vitals ?   On the Somme attrition became at
last a menace to Germany, for it was acute attrition :
not like the slow erosion of cliffs by the sea, but like
the steady crumbling of a mountain to which hydraulic
engineers have applied a mighty head of water.

From July 1st Britain took over the major share of
the fighting on the Western Front.   France in the
year had won great fame, but she had lost a million
men and she was very weary.   The fighting quality
of her sons had been proved beyond dispute, but so
unhappily had the weakness of her High Command.
Her staff work, which the world had been taught
to admire, was faulty both in theory and practice, and
the pre-war doubts of Germany were amply justified.
The realism, which had been its boast, was a blend
of sentimentality and prejudice, and its superficial
logic could no longer conceal its futility.   Those few
of France's soldiers, who were longer sighted and had
the courage of their opinions, were soon discarded.
Before the War ended she was to produce great
leaders, but they were not in high command at the
start.   Most dangerous of all was her General-in-
Chief.   Joffre was the typical French bourgeois, a
soldier expert in the orthodox parts of his profession,
a character stalwart and imperturbable, but suspicious of subordinates and jealous of colleagues,
a mind inelastic and infertile.   At the start his
optimism and rock-like placidity had been valuable
to his country, but the value had gone.   His intellectual mediocrity had become too glaring, and his
supersession was inevitable.

There were no decisive events elsewhere on the long battle-fronts. In the East Brussilov's great summer offensive won much ground and expedited the break-up of Austria ; but he could not develop his success, and his losses of over a million still further lowered the spirit of his own command. It led, however, to the dismissal of Falkenhayn, to the failure of Austria's offensive against Italy, and to the entry into war of Rumania on the Allied side. Rumania made nothing of her tardy resolution. She was presently overrun by Mackensen and put out of action, but her conquest did little to improve Germany's military position, since it lengthened the Eastern Front for her by 250 miles. For the rest the Allies were virtually immobilised at Salonika, and Townshend's army was forced to surrender at Kut in April. The Mesopotamian enterprise ended in disaster, but, considering the nature of the country and our inferiority in numbers and supplies, it had been no disgrace to British arms. The events of the year were a lesson in what could be done under difficulties, if war were conducted not by a loose partnership but by a single and concentrated control. They had brought into supreme power Germany's natural leaders, Hindenburg and Ludendorff, the massive character and the orderly brain. One consequence was that all her resources of production were combined under an iron dictatorship.

On the naval side there befell one event which might have changed the destiny of the world. The British blockade, in spite of difficulties with the United States, had been steadily growing tighter, and the answering German submarine campaign more active. The Grand Fleet in Scottish waters gave little sign of life, nor that hidden behind the bulwark of Heligoland. But the British Navy was winning without striking a blow. Besides the army in France, it and our merchant service were providing for four distant campaigns, and at the same time keeping Britain herself fed and supplied. With the advent of Scheer to high command Germany changed her waiting tactics, and sought to isolate and destroy some portion of the British Grand Fleet. On May 30th it was clear that part of the German Fleet had come out of port, and Beatty with his battle-cruisers was ordered to sweep the eastern part of the North Sea, and then join Jellicoe, who with the Grand Fleet was moving in the north. A casual Danish merchantman drew out ships from both Hipper's and Beatty's battle-cruiser squadrons to inspect it, and so contact between the adversaries was brought about on the afternoon of May 31st.

So began the Battle of Jutland. Beatty, heavily punished by Hipper, turned north and drew him towards Jellicoe. He had escaped from the trap, and now it was the turn of Hipper and Scheer to enter it. The details of what followed will no doubt be debated for centuries ; here we need say only that the two adversaries made contact, that Scheer and Hipper narrowly escaped, and that in a night of gloom the Germans slipped round the British and returned to port with smaller losses than their opponents. Jellicoe had fought the battle which he always intended to fight, taking no undue risks, since he believed that so long as the British Grand Fleet was unbeaten it was victorious. Jutland, the uncompromising details of which were at once published by the British Admiralty, did us no good, but it also did us little harm. In a fog of uncertainty Jellicoe handled the affair ably, and, if he was also cautious, such was not only the nature of the man but the essence of his policy. He could not have destroyed Scheer without taking risks which might have destroyed himself, and with him would have gone down the Allied cause. It was a war of peoples, and even the most resounding triumph at sea would not have ended the contest, while a defeat would have struck from the Allied hands the weapon on which all others depended. If it be argued that such considerations belong to statesmanship rather than to naval tactics, it may be replied that the commander of the British Grand Fleet must be statesman as well as seaman.

A week later the cruiser which was carrying the Secretary of State for War on a mission to Russia, was sunk by a mine west of the Orkneys, and Lord Kitchener went down with it. The news filled his country and the Allied nations with profound sorrow. Labour leaders, trade union delegates, and the patrons of the conscientious objector were as sincere in their mourning as his professional colleagues and the army which he had created. At the time he was beyond doubt the most dominant personality in the Empire, and the foremost of Britain's public servants. Yet in a sense he was fortunate in the hour of his death, for his work was done. In twenty-two months he had expanded six divisions into seventy and made a great army. Now he was living in an unfamiliar atmosphere. He did not understand, nor was he understood by, certain of his colleagues. For politics in the ordinary sense he had no aptitude. After the smooth mastery of his earlier career, he was often puzzled and unhappy in the vortex in which he found himself. His epitaph might well be the words written of a very different figure, but applicable to any career of splendid but incomplete achievement : " A little space was allowed him to show at least a heroic purpose, and attest a high design ; then, with all things unfinished before him and behind, he fell asleep after many troubles and triumphs. Few can ever have gone wearier to the grave ; none with less fear." *

IV

The temper of Britain, as the year 1916 wore to its close, was becoming different both from the excitement of the first months of war and the exasperation and confusion of 1915. We were beginning to learn the meaning of the task we had undertaken. The old civilian fury against the enemy had gone ; the mood of the people had become more like that of the men in the field, in its ironical resignation and the sense that the business was too grave to permit of any " vileinye of hate." The War was no more a reported tale ; enemy aircraft had stricken down men and women in English streets, the life of the trenches could be envisaged by the dullest, and death, which had left few families unbereaved, was becoming once more the supreme uniter.

But this new seriousness and poise must inevitably make a nation more critical. There was a growing belief that the Government was trying to cure an earthquake with small political pills. The Coalition formed in May 1915 had not been a mobilisation of

* Swinburne on Byron.

the best talent of the nation, but a compromise between party interests. Its machinery, too, was not
fitted for the prompt dispatch of business. During
the autumn men of all classes were beginning to ask
themselves whether a Government so constituted
was capable of winning the War. It is probable that
for many months the great majority of the people of
Britain had been convinced that a change was necessary, but the Government was slow to read the
weather signs. Hence, when the blow came, there
was a tendency to attribute it to a malign conspiracy
and a calumnious press. But in the crisis of such a
war no Government could have been driven from
office by backstair intrigues alone or by the most
skilful newspaper cabal. The press which criticised
owed its power solely to the fact that it echoed what
was in most men's minds. The nation felt that the
results achieved were not adequate to its sacrifice or
its spirit.

Mr. Lloyd George was, now as ever, the interpreter
of the subconscious popular mind. Alone of his
Liberal colleagues, he realised that the political
expertise, of which they had been such masters, was
as much in the shadow as the champion faro-player
in a Far Western township which had been visited
by a religious revival. His powerful intelligence
was turned into other channels, and he brought to
the conduct of this war between nations the same
passion which in other days he showed in the strife
between classes. When he succeeded Lord Kitchener
at the War Office he found himself with little
authority ; he was convinced that things were being
mismanaged at the front, and he was determined to
infuse into their conduct a fiercer purpose, and to

win back policy and major strategy to the control of the Cabinet. To do this he must either be Prime Minister himself, or head of a small War Directory which had full executive responsibility. At the close of November he put the latter proposal before Mr. Asquith.

In the beginning of December the matter got into the newspapers. The Conservative leaders, when consulted by Mr. Bonar Law, showed little love for Mr. Lloyd George, but were anxious that Mr. Asquith should resign in order that he might reconstruct his Cabinet ; they themselves were willing to tender their resignations, but it was clear that they hoped that the new Cabinet would not include the War Minister. Mr. Asquith thereupon accepted Mr. Lloyd George's proposal for a small War Committee, of which he should not be a member, but over whose decisions he should have control. But, partly because of an apparently inspired campaign in the press and partly on the advice of his Liberal colleagues, he presently changed his mind and withdrew his consent. Mr. Lloyd George resigned, and Mr. Asquith made the mistake of also resigning, since he believed himself indispensable. The King sent for Mr. Bonar Law, who declared himself unable to construct an administration, and on December 7th Mr. Lloyd George kissed hands as Prime Minister. Owing to the magnanimity of Mr. Balfour, who accepted the Foreign Office though Mr. Lloyd George had long been trying to oust him from the Admiralty, the Conservative statesmen came in, and a Government was duly formed. Its most important feature was a War Cabinet of five—Mr. Lloyd George ; Mr. Bonar Law, the Chancellor of the Exchequer ; Lord

Curzon, the Lord President of the Council ; and, as Ministers without departments, Mr. Arthur Henderson, the Labour leader, and Lord Milner, in whose political faith imperialism was joined to wide dreams of social reconstruction.

It is easy to criticise the whole business—to point out, for example, that Mr. Lloyd George became president of the War Cabinet while in his first proposal he had insisted that the Prime Minister should not be a member of it. The momentous transformation was no doubt tarnished by intrigue and personal ambition, and by much ungraciousness in the manner of it. Mr. Asquith and Sir Edward Grey, who had laboured long in the service of their country, retired to the accompaniment of coarse abuse from a section of the press. Yet beyond question the change was necessary, and it had behind it the assent of a people not careless of the decencies. That new leaders should be demanded in a strife which affects national existence is as natural as the changes of the seasons. Few men are so elastic in mind that, having given all their strength to one set of problems, they can turn with unabated vigour to new needs and new conditions. The nation, again, must be able to view its masters with hopefulness, and in all novelty there is hope. There was that, too, in the temperament and talents of the Prime Minister himself upon which men had begun to look coldly. He left on the ordinary mind the impression that he thought more of argument than of action. It seemed to his critics impossible to expect the unresting activity and the bold origination which the situation required from one whose habits of thought and deed were cast in the more leisurely mould of an older school of statesmen.

When a people judges there is usually reason in
its verdict, and it is idle to argue that Mr. Asquith
was a perfect, or even the best available, leader in
war-time. But history will not let his qualities go
unacclaimed. He had admirable nerve and courage,
and as a consequence he was the most loyal of colleagues, for he never shrank from accepting the
burden of his own mistakes and those of his subordinates. He was incapable of intrigue in any form.
He had true personal dignity, caring little for either
abuse or praise, and shunning the arts of self-advertise-
ment. And if his optimism had at times an unfortunate effect, there can be no doubt that his coolness and patience did much to keep an even temper
in the people during months of disappointment and
darkness. History will see in him a great parlia-
mentarian, a great public servant, and a great
gentleman.

CHAPTER III

THE SALLIES

UP till now the War had been fought largely
on traditional methods, by combatants whose
national integration was still intact. But with 1917
a change came over the scene. Ancient constitutions
began to crack, old faiths to be questioned, potent,
undreamed-of powers to be released. Everywhere in
the world was heard the sound of things breaking.

In half-conscious anticipation of this change there
began a fumbling movement towards peace. The
wiser heads in every country were coming to fear
that their peoples might crumble through sheer
weariness, and that absolute victory, even if it were
won, might only mean absolute chaos. The first
move came from Germany, but her peace offer of
December 1916 was framed in the arrogant terms
of one who felt that she held the winning cards. Her
main motive was prudential. The Somme had shown
her that her military machine was being strained to
breaking-point ; if it broke all would be over, and
at any cost that catastrophe must be averted. If the
belligerents consented to treat, she believed that she
had certain advantages in any conference. She had
much to give up which she could not hold, and her
renunciation might win her the things she considered
vital for her future. Moreover, once her opponents
were entangled in discussion, there was a chance of

breaking up their unity and shifting the argument
to minor issues. It was a matter of life and death
to her that a rift should appear in the Allied lute
before she suffered any irremediable disaster. She
had also an eye on neutral states, especially America,
who would not be likely to welcome a summary
bolting of the door against negotiations. Finally,
there was a tactical motive. She was contemplating
new and anarchic methods of naval warfare, and to
justify herself she had to appear as an angel of peace
who had been rudely repulsed. Action which pro-
ceeds from so many mixed reasons is apt to blunder,
and the impression left by the German overtures
on men's minds was one of maladroitness carried to
the pitch of genius. The reply of the Allies on
December 30th exposed their emptiness, and the
German Chancellor at long last assented to the policy
of unrestricted submarine warfare which was to
come very near being the end of Britain.

The effects of the War were so catastrophic and
terrible that the historian, looking back, is not inclined
to be contemptuous of any effort to end it. But it
is clear that the German offer was impossible. There
was more hope in the overtures of Austria, whose
new Emperor Charles, through the medium of his
brother-in-law, Prince Sixtus of Bourbon, made secret
proposals for a separate peace. They shipwrecked
principally upon the opposition of Italy and France,
whose reply was that of Lucio's comrade in *Measure
for Measure*—" Heaven grant us its peace, but not
the King of Hungary's ! "

Nor could there be any practical issue from President Wilson's offer of mediation in the closing months
of 1916. He had just been re-elected as a peace-

President, but he saw the clouds thickening ahead, and he felt that he must be able to justify himself to his people if he were forced to a course which was not pacific. He asked for a definition of war aims— " that soundings be taken in order that we may learn, the neutral nations with the belligerents, how near the haven of peace may be for which all mankind longs." The Allied Governments, in spite of a certain irritation among their peoples, had the wit to see Mr. Wilson's purpose. In a remarkable document they set forth patiently and temperately, not indeed their war aims in detail, since these could not be formulated till the hour for negotiation arrived, but their general purpose, which was wholly consistent with American ideals. Nearly two years before the coming of peace they stated almost all the principles on which that peace was founded.

I

Alone of the Allies Britain had now attained a certain unity in the direction of the War, for she had a Prime Minister who could draw together and maximise all the powers of the nation. Mr. Lloyd George's pre-War record had shown that he had unsurpassed demagogic talents, and that rarer gift, a sense of political atmosphere. He might err in his ultimate judgments, but rarely in his immediate intuitions ; if his strategy was often erroneous, his tactics were seldom at fault. His interest was not in doctrine but in life, and his quick sense of reality made him at heart an opportunist—one who loved the gross persistency of facts, and was prepared to select, if need be, from the repertory of any party.

This elasticity, combined with his high political courage, had made him even in his bitterest campaigns not wholly repugnant to his opponents, for he was always human, and had none of the dogmatic rigidity, the lean spiritual pride, of the elder Liberalism.

Now he had found his proper task, and was emerging as one of the most formidable figures in the world. Lord Milner, who had historical perspective and did not praise unadvisedly, considered him the greatest War Minister since Chatham. He was a born coalitionist, sitting always loose to parties, a born War Minister, since strife was his element, and a born leader of a democracy. Of democracy, indeed, both in its strength and weakness, he was more than a representative—he was a personification. He had its fatal facility in general ideas, its sentimentality, its love of picturesque catchwords ; and he had also its incongruous realism in action. Devotees of consistency were distressed by his vagaries, for a tyrant or an oligarchy may be consistent, but not a free people. He had a democracy's short memory, and its brittle personal loyalties. Perhaps his supreme merit as a popular leader was his comprehensibility. No mystery surrounded his character or his talents. The qualities and defects of both were evident to all, and the plain man found in them something which he could himself assess—positive merits, positive weaknesses, so that he could give or withhold his confidence as if he were dealing with a familiar. This power of diffusing a personality, of producing a sense of intimacy among millions who have never seen his face or heard his voice, is the greatest of assets for a democratic statesman, and Mr. Lloyd George had it not only for Britain but for all the world.

His character and mind were curiously of a piece. He had no petty vulgarities in his composition, though he was shrewdly aware of them in others and knew how to use them ; he was good-humoured and friendly ; he had little personal vanity, for the monotonous infallibility of his later *Memoirs* does not fairly represent the man in his great days. Lacking the normal education of British public servants, he had large gaps in his mental furniture, and consequently was without that traditional sense of proportion which often gives an air of wisdom to mediocrities. He had a unique power of assimilating knowledge, but not an equal power of retaining it. Hence his mental processes were somewhat lacking in continuity ; all was atomic and episodic, rather than a steady light. His mind had in it little of the scientific, it was insensitive to guiding principles, and here was no even diffusion of its power through many channels.

But his virtues were to a notable degree the qualities of his defects. The lack of ordinary knowledge saved him from the dominion of the ordinary platitudes. The fact that his mind was not a *continuum*, as the phrase goes, but a thing discrete and perpetually re-made, kept him from lassitude and staleness. The world to which he woke each morning was a new birth of time, to be faced with all the interest of the pioneer. And the fact that one subject must at the moment exclude all others gave him in that one subject a tremendous velocity, that one-idea-ed concentration which is a most formidable weapon in war. His loose hold on principles kept him from formalism, and opportunism is often the right attitude in a crisis. The whole combination—limited knowledge, limitless ardour, absorption in the task of the moment, adventurous interest—spelled that first of virtues in a War Minister, *courage de tête*, fearlessness in the face of a swiftly changing world. He did not ask to see a map of the road, but he was prepared without reservation to grapple with any and all of the terrors of pilgrimage.

As the months passed, critics were found to depreciate his wisdom, his honesty, even his talents, but none ever denied his vitality. His physical appearance was a clue to the man ; the thick-set figure, the deep chest, the bright, wary swordsman's eye—all spoke of ebullient and inexhaustible life. He was exhilarated rather than depressed by misfortune, even though he might be also a little scared. His strength was that he overflowed at all times with zest and interest and fervour. The Allied cause now made the same appeal to him that the handicaps and sufferings of the poor had made in earlier days. He was not only energetic himself but an inspirer of energy in others, for, like a gadfly, he stung all his environment to life. Many of his endowments, such as his parliamentary tact, his subtlety in the management of colleagues, his debating skill, even that eloquence which at its best was a noble poetry, however invaluable to a statesman in normal times, were of less account in war. But that one gift he had which is so rare and inexplicable that it may rightly be called genius. In the darkest days his vitality soared above the fog and made a kind of light by its very ardour. He might be himself impatient of the long view and the wise course, but the magnetic effluence was there to inspire sager heads and not less resolute hearts. He could not be defeated, because his spirit of buoyancy and zeal was insatiable, and therefore unconquerable, and that spirit he communicated to the nation.

The machine which he fashioned, the War Cabinet, worked on the whole with vigour, if not always with precision. Much was due to its secretary, Sir Maurice Hankey, who in every circumstance of the War showed an uncanny foresight and a supreme competence. The special executive duties fell chiefly on two men. One was General Smuts, who in a certain kind of informal diplomacy had no equal, and who was in consequence often charged with impossible missions. The other was Lord Milner, who from the start of the War Cabinet bore the weight of its most difficult tasks. He was the ablest living British administrator, and no more powerful intellect and purer and more resolute character have been devoted in our time to the public service. Caring nothing for popularity and without oratorical gifts, he was by a fortunate chance in most things the natural complement of the Prime Minister.

If a further proof be needed of Mr. Lloyd George's miraculous vitality, it will be found in the fact that he could spare interest for matters which extended beyond the fortunes of the War. He made the War Cabinet a council of the whole Empire by summoning to its special meetings representatives of India and of the Dominions. Well might the Prime Minister of Canada declare that this meant the writing of a new page in imperial history. If it be said that there was a war purpose in such a step, since the whole Empire was in arms, and a war purpose in a measure like the Corn Production Act, which opened up a new vista for British agriculture, there could be

none in the inquiries which Mr. Lloyd George set
afoot and which resulted in Mr. Fisher's great
Education Bill, and the drastic scheme of electoral
reform which admitted women to the vote, and the
inception of the Whitley Councils. Under the pressure
of war the old individualism of industry was breaking
down, the State was enlarging its sphere of interest
and duty, and on some there broke the vision of a
new and wiser world coming to birth while the old
things were dying.

II

The first of the old things to die was the Tsarist
regime in Russia. A *coup d'état*, supported by most
of the troops, ended on March 16th 1917 with the
abdication of the Tsar and the establishment of a
provisional Government. But the revolution was
only beginning. The Liberal intellectuals now in
office believed that they could conduct both a revolution and a war. They were soon undeceived, for it
was against the War that the revolution was aimed.
Kerensky, an emotional Girondin, who became Chief
Minister, flung his energies into a great Russian
offensive, but all discipline had gone from the army,
and the last Russian attack of July 1st miserably
failed. After that events marched fast. Outlaws long
in exile were assisted by Germany to return to their
native land, and among them came that strange
being, Vladmir Ulianov, familiar to the world as
Lenin, who was to be the Messiah of a new gospel.
He and his Bolsheviks, knowing precisely what they
wanted, prevailed against a leader who believed that
rhetoric could hold a starving and dispirited people.
The army ceased to be an orderly force, and became

a mob of peasants, clamouring for bread, for peace, and for land. Throughout the summer Kerensky laboured at his hopeless task, while the underground forces were growing stronger. Then Germany struck, and Riga fell ; Kornilov, the one fighting general left, wasted his strength in futile quarrels ; a weary people turned to whatever offered leadership ; and in October the Bolshevik revolution, inspired by Lenin and organised by Trotsky, marched swiftly to power. On November 7th its triumph was complete, the triumph of a handful of determined men. An armistice soon followed, and at Brest Litovsk before the close of the year the new Russian rulers accepted from Germany a degrading peace.

Such is the bare record of a great tragedy. The tragedy was for the Russian people, who against terrible handicaps had struggled for two years with patient heroism, and were now condemned to a more horrible carnival of famine and blood ; not for the Tsarist regime, which most amply deserved its fate. It had become an anachronism in the modern world, a mediæval fragment in line neither with the blundering German absolutism nor with the freedom of the Western peoples. History can only regard the gentle, ineffective, tragically-fated Emperor with compassion. He was born to a destiny too difficult ; his very virtues—his loyalty, his mercifulness—contributed to his undoing. The worst influence was the wife whom he deeply loved, and who so surrounded him with rogues and charlatans that his Court stank in the nostrils of decent citizens. The autocracy collapsed from its own inherent rottenness. The old order crumbled at the first challenge, for it had become mere lath and plaster.

Russia's revolution, unlike the French, had not come from the burning inspiration of a new faith, but from sheer weariness of mind and body, from utter loss of nerve and heart. There had always been in her people a certain lack of bone and fibre ; as someone has said, they had the courage to die, but not to live. She had never wholly emerged from the servile state, and she was now to experience another type of serfdom. For upon her enfeebled frame a new faith fastened like a leech. The Bolsheviks were a mere fraction of the people, and they had many diverse types among them, but they owed unswerving allegiance to Lenin—the squat, smiling figure with the contemptuous eyes, who was known to admit that in every hundred of his followers only one was a true believer, and that of the residue sixty were fools and thirty-nine knaves. They were class maniacs, and in their own eyes class martyrs, and their day of revenge had come. They would liberate not only from the last shackles of Tsardom, but from the tumid constitutionalism beloved by the pedants of the West.

They were Marxists, but not orthodox Marxists, for they claimed a right to a free interpretation of their master. Capitalism was to disappear, and in the single-class community the co-operation of all would take the place of exploitation by the few. But before the unfeatured desert of their ideal could be attained rough places must be crossed, and the method must be a temporary dictatorship, the dictatorship of the workers, till capitalists and bourgeois were forcibly eliminated—converted or destroyed. Toleration was unthinkable, a synonym for weakness : the majority rule of democracy was equally impossible, for communists would never be a majority till they had purged the State by civil war. They were resolved to simplify society with the knife ; a small elect minority, they would force the rest to do their bidding, because they were prepared to go to any lengths of terror and crime. It was class-rule carried to its logical conclusion, and murder exalted to be a normal function of the State. In this nightmare certain categories of Western thought made unholy alliance with the dark fatalism and the ancient cruelties of the East.

Beyond the Atlantic a second thing broke down, America's patience and her traditional isolation. On February 1st Germany entered upon unrestricted submarine warfare, proclaiming a state of blockade in all the approaches to Europe, and her intention to sink at sight any vessel whatsoever found in those waters. The German Ambassador at Washington was promptly given his passports, but it was not till five American vessels were sunk in March with loss of life, and secret overtures were discovered from Germany to Mexico, that Mr. Wilson took action. On April 2nd the President asked Congress for a declaration of war. He outlined means for the preparation of America and for supplying the Allies with what they needed, and he concluded almost in the strain of Lincoln's Second Inaugural :

It is a fearful thing to lead this great and peaceful people into war. . . . But the right is more precious than peace, and we shall fight for the things we have always carried nearest our hearts—for democracy, for the right of those who submit to authority to have a voice in their own government, for the rights and liberties of small nations, for the universal dominion of right by such a concert of free peoples as shall bring peace and safety to all nations and make the world itself at last free. To such a task we can dedicate our lives and our fortunes, everything that we are and everything that we have, with the pride of those who know that the day has come when America is privileged to spend her blood and her might for the principles that gave her birth and happiness and the peace that she has treasured. God helping her, she can do no other.

With a strong people a slow change is a sure change. America flung herself into the preparations for war with a disciplined enthusiasm. Her coming seemed to make victory certain and the right kind of victory, for she entered upon war not for any parochial ends, but for the reorganisation of the world's life on a sane basis. She brought with her enormous assets. She was the largest workshop on earth ; she had immense wealth to put into the common stock ; she had a powerful fleet and a great capacity for shipbuilding ; her reserves of man-power made her army capable of almost unlimited expansion. Mr. Wilson's achievement should not be forgotten. He had brought the whole nation into line on a matter which meant the reversal of every traditional mode of thought : and one who remembers the centrifugal tendencies of American life and its stiff conservatism must admit that such a feat demanded no small genius in statecraft.

But during these months there was another thing in danger of breaking—a thing whose destruction would have condemned the Allies to defeat long before America could take the field. Germany in her new submarine campaign had calculated that in five or six months she could bring Britain to her knees by cutting off sea-borne supplies. She was beginning herself to realise that in the long run the home front was the vital front. For a little it looked as if her calculations were right. She had five times as many submarines as in 1915, and she made ample use of them. In the closing months of 1916 the average loss of British tonnage had been 300,000 : in February 1917 it rose to 468,000 ; in March to 500,000, and in April to 875,000. In the last month all our western sea approaches became a cemetery, and one ship out of four that left British ports never returned. Only six weeks' supply of corn remained in the country.

It was the darkest moment in the War for Britain, but it was not realised except by the Government and the Admiralty. The Prime Minister rose to the crisis. It was impossible to reply by an offensive —by laying a mine-field close to the German bases, or by attacking these bases, for Jutland had left us without the full command of the North Sea. Much was done by rationing, by increasing home production, and by expanding our shipbuilding, but the real remedy, which before the summer was gone relieved the situation, was a new plan of defence. The convoy system was pressed upon an unwilling Admiralty—let it be said in fairness that at the time we had not the promise of a multitude of American destroyers—and with the help of some of the younger naval officers it was finally accepted and put into force. It worked like a charm. The losses to convoyed ships were only one per cent., and by September the monthly tonnage lost was under 200,000. When peace came 88,000 merchant vessels had been convoyed with a loss of only 436. Moreover, by various devices life was made more precarious for the enemy submarines. By the end of the War more than half of the German U-boats had been destroyed, all but a handful by the British Navy.

III

The new Government in Britain attempted to
infuse its own spirit of vigour into the land campaign. But there it found itself confronted with a
tougher problem. Mr. Lloyd George had never
believed in the dogma of his military advisers that the
Western Front was the only decisive area. He did
not greatly believe in soldiers, since he distrusted all
hierarchies and was constitutionally disinclined to
submit to the dictation of experts. He thought, not
without reason, that, since they were engaged in
a new kind of war, the ordinary staff officers had
little to their credit except a certain familiarity with
an out-of-date technique. He was blind to the
gains of the Somme battles, but he was acutely
alive to their cost. He could see small co-ordination in the many desperate Allied attacks of the
past two years. When he was told that they had
a common purpose, the attrition of the enemy, he
replied that attrition in the third year of war could
not be a serious policy, but a confession of the absence
of a policy. If we were wearing Germany down we
were wearing ourselves out of existence, and com-
peting in a futile race towards bankruptcy.

His instinct was right, but it was not easy to find
means to enforce it. He still hankered after a
switching of the main attack to a flank, and early in
1917 leaned to the sending of large bodies of troops
to the Italian front for a knock-out blow against
Austria. But it is doubtful if at this stage of the campaign such a transference was possible, since the
two main forces had become *accrochés,* hooked together

on the front in the West. Nor was his first effort to obtain some central direction more happily inspired, for it meant putting Haig and his army in a quasi-subordination to Nivelle, the new French Commander-in-Chief. But it is only fair to recognise the soundness of the instinct which inspired these adventures. Of all the civilians I have known Mr. Lloyd George seems to me to have possessed in the highest degree the capacity for becoming a great soldier. But he might have lost several armies while he was learning his trade.

In November 1916 a conference at Chantilly had laid down the French and British plans for the coming year. It was agreed that the main burden must fall on the British Army. The chief effort was to be an attack by it north of the Somme, and by the French south of the Oise, with a subsidiary movement in Champagne, to be followed in the summer by a British advance towards the enemy bases on the Belgian coast. Nivelle's advent changed all this. He decided to confine Haig to the Arras region, and to deliver himself a mighty assault on the Aisne plateau. His purpose was not a series of methodical advances, but a complete break-through and a limitless pursuit. Haig and Pétain were sceptical, but he secured the approval of the two Governments, for to the civilians this seemed to be at any rate something more hopeful than the weary *guerre d'usure.*

Germany intervened to dislocate the plan. Ludendorff, aware of his diminishing man-power, set himself to reorganise his armies, and to prepare the way for that victory on land which he believed must follow the submarine triumph. Across the chord of his great salient in the west from Lens to Rheims he built a gigantic series of defences, which were named after the heroes of German mythology, and which Britain knew as the Hindenburg Line. Then he withdrew his front towards it, devastating all the area relinquished. It was a wise and provident plan, perfectly executed. It gave Germany a shorter and far stronger line. Above all it delayed and compromised the Allies' offensive. They could not now strike before April, and Germany, instead of being pinned down, as Haig desired, to an awkward position, had a margin for refitment and rest.

The tale of the Allied campaign that year—in the West, for there was presently no Eastern Front—is one of difficult beginnings, successes which led nowhere, and desperate battles which all but broke their hearts. On April 9th Haig opened at Arras, captured the Vimy Ridge (which was to prove an invaluable gain in a year's time), and was compelled to continue long after attack was fruitless. For meanwhile, on April 16th, Nivelle struck on the Aisne, with a poor tactical scheme and no chance of surprise, since the enemy knew his plans in detail. He suffered a costly check. For a little it seemed that the strength of France might melt away, since mutiny ran through the army, and at one moment it was believed that there were only two loyal divisions between the enemy and Paris. Pétain restored confidence and order—it was the greatest achievement of a fine soldier ; but it took him all summer to nurse his armies back to health, and meantime Britain had to bear unaided the brunt of the war. At Messines in June we carried out a perfect model of a limited advance—it has been rightly described as the only true siege-warfare attack made throughout a siege war. But Britain could not rest ; it had been the word of the British Prime Minister himself, at the conference in Paris in May which put new hope into France, that no respite must be given to the enemy. Haig turned to the offensive towards the Belgian coast, which had always been his main plan.

This is not the place to tell the melancholy story of that battle of a hundred days which is known as Passchendaele or Third Ypres. There was some merit in its conception, but little in its execution ; the weather early made success impossible, and it was continued long after the mud-holes and ridges aimed at had lost all strategical meaning. The German defence showed great tactical ingenuity, but their strength was strained to its utmost and their fangs against France were for the moment drawn, since this cruellest action of the war cost them 300,000 men, if it cost us 100,000 more. Whatever the reason for the tragic prolongation—the uneasiness of the French, the inelasticity of our military machine—one alleged cause may be ruled out, the personal vanity of Haig. Such was not the nature of the most modest and single-hearted of men.

While our troops were dying in the Flanders bogs the usual autumnal sacrifice of an ally was all but consummated. On October 24th on the middle Isonzo an army of nine Austrian divisions and six German burst in the misty morning through the Italian front, and in a fortnight's fighting forced it back from river line to river line with a loss of 600,000 men. Eventually standing ground was found on the Piave, which covered, but only just covered, Venice. Britain and France sent reinforcements, and British and French generals assisted in reconstituting the broken forces of Italy. Meantime at Cambrai on November 20th Britain, by the use of some 400 tanks, at last achieved a surprise, and for a moment almost brought back the war of manœuvre. The fatal drain of Passchendaele had depleted our reserves, and we were unable to develop our initial victory, or to prevent a vigorous German counter-stroke ten days later. Our reach had exceeded our grasp : yet Cambrai remains one of the key actions of the War, for it offered us a way of release from siege bondage which, after some fumbling, we were to follow. For the first time we learned the true value of the new weapon of which we were the exponents.

We were pioneers at Cambrai in new tactics, of which, fortunately for us, the enemy did not grasp the meaning. But he, too, had been fruitful in tactical novelties. His problem was to discover a method which would restore open warfare and give a decision, and he deserves all credit for a brilliant departure from routine, a true intellectual effort to rethink the main problem of modern war. All former offensives had after a shorter or longer time come to a halt for the same reason—wearied troops were met by fresh reserves. The attacker continued hammering at an unbreakable front, because he had set the stage for action in that one area, and could not easily shift his batteries and communications. In a word, all offensives lacked mobility. Germany's first business, therefore, was to make the battle mobile and bring in the element of surprise.

Her plan was not a break-through in the older sense, but a general crumbling. It was based upon the highly specialised training of certain units, and the absence of any preliminary massing near the point of attack. Again, there was no long bombardment to alarm the enemy. The advance was made by picked troops in small clusters, carrying light trench-mortars and many machine-guns, with the field batteries close behind them in support. The actual mode of attack, which the French called " infiltration," may be likened to a hand, of which the finger-tips are shod with steel, and which is pushed into a yielding substance. The picked troops at the finger ends made gaps through which others passed, till each section of the defence found itself outflanked and encircled. It was no case of an isolated stroke, but of a creeping sickness which might demoralise a hundred miles of front. The first experiment was made at the capture of Riga in September, but the true test came in October at Caporetto. The final proof was the counter-stroke at Cambrai. There the attack on the British left, carried out in the old fashion, signally failed, while the assault on the British right, after the new fashion, as signally succeeded. But the Allied Staffs were slow to grasp the meaning of the new method. Caporetto was explained by a breakdown in Italian nerve, and Cambrai by defective local intelligence. Four months later the armies of France and England read the true lesson in letters of fire.

IV

After Passchendaele and Caporetto some inquisition into military methods was inevitable. The first changes were at British Headquarters. The Prime Minister would fain have seen an alteration in the chief command, but Haig would not be forced from his place, though certain lesser resignations were compelled, much to the advantage of his staff's efficiency. But he made a bold bid for more unity in command. After Caporetto it was decided that a War Council should sit at Versailles, consisting of the Prime Minister and one other statesman from each of the Allies, with four military delegates to act as advisers. The soldiers objected naturally to being mere advisers without executive power, and in January 1918 a revised machinery was framed— a military Committee with Foch as president, empowered to create a general reserve by contributions from the Allied armies. The device had few merits. The same authority that controls general operations must control reserves, and a committee cannot with success command an army—these are elementary principles in war. But the scheme was never tried, for it shipwrecked upon Haig, who, when asked to allocate divisions to the reserve, refused, since he believed that he had none to give.

The controversy led to the resignation of Sir William Robertson, who was succeeded as Chief of the Imperial General Staff by Sir Henry Wilson. Robertson had done valuable work in creating the new British Army, but it was his misfortune to be the sole conduit between two much abler men, neither of whom he could interpret to the other. He could not expound Haig's mind to Mr. Lloyd George or the Prime Minister's mind to Haig. This unfortunate lack of contact was the cause of misunderstandings for which neither party was altogether to blame. The Prime Minister at the time was wrong on many points. His view that the Western Front was " over insured " was wrong : his proposal for a great Palestine offensive was in the circumstances a dangerous folly ; he was wrong as to the Versailles machinery, wrong in his anticipation of Germany's plans, wrong in his starving of Haig and the impossible task which he laid on him. But there is something to be said on his side. He saw the danger of disunion and proposed a remedy ; it was a faulty one, but the soldiers contented themselves with criticising. If in the beginning of 1918 Haig and Robertson had demanded a Generalissimo and had proposed Foch, they would certainly have carried their point, in spite of the Prime Minister's declaration of the previous November. He might fairly have complained that he did not get sufficient help from his official military advisers, and he turned naturally to the fertile, if fantastic, mind of Sir Henry Wilson. In a democracy relations between soldiers and statesmen must always be delicate, but they were notably less strained in Britain than in France or Italy. The War Cabinet never interfered with Haig as Jefferson Davis interfered with Lee before Fredericksburg, and as Lincoln interfered with every Northern general save Grant.

At the close of the third year, for British opinion the outline of the War, which had seemed clear and firm, was now blurred again. Russia had fallen out of line, and new and unknown quantities had entered the problem. It had been a depressing year, which, beginning with the promise of a decision, had closed for the Allies in a deep uncertainty. They had won no indisputable successes except in remote lands ; the taking of Bagdad and Jerusalem affected only Turkey, and while it weakened her extremities did not strike at her heart. Discomfort was growing in every British home, since lights were darkened and rations were reduced, and there was the unvarying tale of losses to rend the heart. The Russian Revolution, followed by the Stockholm Conference, let loose a flood of theorising ; there were incessant disputes with Labour, war-weary, puzzled, suspicious, poisoned to some extent by false propaganda. All zest and daylight had gone out of the struggle. The cause for which we had entered it was now half forgotten, for men's minds had grown numb. Civilians at home, as well as soldiers in the field, felt themselves in the grip of an inexorable machine.

It was a dangerous mood—dangerous to the enemy, for it meant that grim shutting of the teeth which with Britain is a formidable thing. But it was dangerous also to ourselves, for it might have resulted in a coarsening of fibre and a blindness to the longer view and the greater issues. That this was not its consequence was in large part due to the King, who by his visits to every industrial centre kept before dazed and weary minds the greatness of the national purpose and the unity of the people. Wherever he went he seemed to unseal the founts of human sympathy. He visited the Clyde, the Tyne, and most of the chief munition works ; and, to the disquiet of the War Cabinet, he went to Lancashire during a strike and was most royally welcomed. Let me set down his Prime Minister's tribute : " The loyalty of the people was heartened and encouraged . . . by the presence of their Sovereign in their midst, and by the warm personal interest he showed in their work and their anxieties. In estimating the value of the different factors which conduced to the maintenance of our home front in 1917, a very high place must be given to the affection inspired by the

King, and the unremitting diligence with which he set himself in those dark days to discharge the functions of his high office." To the workers he seemed to come not only as monarch but as comrade, with the words of Richard II on his lips : " I live with bread like you, feel want, taste grief, need friends."

V

With the coming of 1918 the initiative passed to the enemy. Russia's collapse enabled him to put larger forces on the Western Front than the Allies could muster. They had resigned themselves to a defensive campaign till America could send her armies ; it was Germany's purpose before that date to reach a decision in the field. It was her last chance. The submarine campaign had failed, and daily the menace from beyond the Atlantic drew nearer. Her people were weak with privations and sick with hope deferred. A little longer and their wonderful fortitude would break. With all the strength she could muster, with her new tactics to aid her, and with a desperate necessity to goad her, she undertook the last great sally and staked everything on victory.

Ludendorff's general plan was to isolate the British Army, roll it up from its right, and drive it into the sea, or pin it down to an entrenched camp between the Somme and the Channel—a Torres Vedras from which it would emerge only on the signature of peace. This done, he could hold it with few troops, swing round on the French, and put them out of action. He must strike, therefore, with all his might at the point of junction of Haig and Pétain, on the western face of the great salient, where

183

the Allies were weakest and the ground easiest. His
position on interior lines gave him the chance of
surprise, for till the actual attack the Allies would
not know on which side of the salient the blow was
to fall. His admirable communications would enable
him to obtain a great local predominance. For the
first stage of the battle he had sixty-three divisions
in line or in immediate reserve.

The Versailles Council miscalculated both the place
and the date of the attack. Haig's Intelligence service informed him of the exact hour, but he had
neither the time nor the resources to prepare an
adequate defence. He held 130 miles of line, and
these the most critical in the West, with approximately
the same numbers as he had had two years before,
when his front was only 80 miles long and Russia
was still in the field. An initial German success was
almost predestined. Nineteen divisions in line and
thirteen in reserve can scarcely stand against a first
attacking wave of thirty-seven divisions, which was
presently to grow to sixty-three.

This most perilous stage for the British Army—and,
except for the First Marne, the most perilous for the
Allied cause—opened in the fog of the early morning
of March 21st, when at a quarter to five four
thousand German guns were released against the
British front, while all the back areas were drenched
with gas, which hung like a pall in the moist air.
The fortnight of the Somme retreat cannot be told
in a simple Homeric narrative ; it was a medley of
confused operations, improvised plans, chances, mis-
chances, and incredible heroisms. On the first day
forty miles of the British line were submerged, and,
in a week, forty miles off the enemy tide was lapping

the walls of Amiens. Ludendorff achieved much, but he did not achieve his main purpose, for by April 5th the battle had died down, Amiens was not taken, the front had been restored, and the French and British were not separated. This failure was due to many causes ; he was false to the spirit of his own tactics, and, instead of exploiting weakness when he had found it, wasted his strength on the steadfast bastion of Arras ; half-way through he fumbled, forgot his true aim, and became the hasty improviser. Perhaps he sought to achieve the impossible, for his troops outmarched their supplies and their stamina, and, accustomed to short commons, lost discipline often when they found Allied stores to plunder. Yet he won a notable victory, and, to the ultimate advantage of the Allies, was encouraged to continue, for, had his blow been parried at the start, he might have relapsed on the defensive, and thereby protracted the War.

The British Army had written a shining page in its history, for a retreat may be as glorious as an advance. By the end of March seventy-three German divisions had engaged thirty-seven British. The disparity was in reality far greater than two to one, for, owing to the German power of local concentration, in many parts of the field the odds had been three or four to one. After the second day we had no prepared lines on which to retire, and the rivers parallel to our front were useless from the drought. It was a marvel that our gossamer front wavered and blew in the wind but never wholly disappeared. Again and again complete disaster was miraculously averted. Scratch forces held up storm troops ; cavalry did work that no cavalry had ever done before in the history of war ; gunners broke every rule of the textbooks. The retreat was in flat defiance of all precedent and law, and it succeeded only because of the stubborn value of the British soldier.

The moment was too solemn for half-measures. A divided command could not defend the long, lean front of the Allies against Germany's organised might, directed by a single brain towards a single purpose. One strong hand must be on the helm, and one only. On March 23rd Haig, after seeing Pétain, telegraphed to London for the Chief of the Imperial General Staff. At the request of the Prime Minister Lord Milner also crossed the Channel on the 24th, and on the 26th he and Sir Henry Wilson met Clemenceau and Poincaré, Haig, Foch and Pétain at Doullens. This conference, held amid the backwash of the great retreat, was in a sense the turning point of the war. The proposal for a supreme commander-in-chief, urged by Milner and supported by Clemenceau, was accepted by Pétain and welcomed by Haig, and for the post Foch was unanimously chosen. The Allies in their extremity turned with one accord to the slight, grizzled, deep-eyed man of sixty-six, who during a laborious lifetime had made himself a master of war.

The ordeal was the source of other blessings. America increased her recruiting, and strained every nerve to quicken the dispatch of troops, so that she might soon stand in line with her allies. Mr. Lloyd George and M. Clemenceau appealed to President Wilson, and no appeal was ever more generously met. General Pershing postponed his plan of a separate American section of operations, and offered to Foch every man, gun and lorry which America had in Europe. France showed that quiet and almost prosaic resolution to win or perish which two years before had inspired her troops at Verdun. In Britain the threat of industrial strikes disappeared, and of their own accord the workers gave up their Easter holiday in order to make up by an increased output for lost guns and stores. On April 10th the House of Commons passed by a large majority a Bill raising the limit of military age to fifty, and giving the Government power to abolish the ordinary exemptions. Divisions were transferred from Palestine and Salonika to France, the old precautions against invasion were dropped, and, within a month from March 21st, 355,000 men were sent across the Channel.

But when the King visited his armies in France in the last days of March the situation was still on a razor's edge. He had gone to them for a week during the flood-tide of the Somme battles ; he had visited them again, accompanied by the Queen, on the eve of Passchendaele. Now he went to them in the throes of their sternest trial. He saw remnants of battalions which had been through the retreat, and he saw units which in a week or two were to be engaged in the not less desperate stand on the Lys. The battle-field was a solemn place, for already we had lost more men than in the whole thirty-four weeks of the Dardanelles campaign. The King's visit was an appeal to his troops to " take counsel from the valour of their hearts," an appeal which Haig, the least rhetorical of men, was a fortnight later to put into grave and memorable words :

There is no other course but to fight it out. Every position must be held to the last man ; there must be no retirement. With our backs to the wall, and believing in the justice of our cause, each one of us must fight on to the end. The safety of our homes and the freedom of mankind depend alike upon the conduct of each one of us at this critical moment.

187

CHAPTER IV

SURRENDER

I

ON April 1st came Ludendorff's second blow. Originally designed as a mere diversion, it grew by its startling success into a major effort, and thereby further compromised his main strategy. His aim was to push through between La Bassée and Armentières, and then, pressing north-west, to capture Hazebrouck and the hills beyond Bailleul. This would mean a general British retirement and a direct threat to Calais and Boulogne, and would eat up the Allied reserves. It achieved that indeed, but it also ate up his own. In three days he had advanced eleven miles, and for a week and more there was a stern resistance against odds. Foch, by his delay in sending help, tried Haig's patience high, but the issue proved that he was wise. The British front sagged and bent but it held, and by the end of April Ludendorff realised that he must try elsewhere.

He was becoming desperate ; his original strategical scheme had gone, and his efforts were now in the nature of a gambler's throw. On May 27th the new storm broke on the Aisne heights, and by the evening the French gains in three great actions had vanished like smoke, and the enemy was across the river. On the second day he was beyond the Vesle, and on the third his vanguard was looking down from the heights of the Tardenois on the waters of the Marne. It was the swiftest advance made in the West since the beginning of trench warfare. But Ludendorff could turn it to no account. He tried to press westward and failed ; on June 9th he tried to cut off the Allied salient between the two great dents which he had made, and failed again. His position was brilliant but without hope. He was the victim of his own successes.

His last offensive came on July 15th, east and west of Rheims. It achieved nothing, for, though the enemy crossed the Marne, it was only to enter the Allied trap. Hitherto Foch had stood patiently on the defensive, hoarding his assets. He had tried almost too highly the fortitude of the British soldier. Now he had got his reserve, and Haig, to augment it, had, to the consternation of the War Cabinet, dangerously thinned his own front in the north. The moment had come to use it. On July 18th he struck at the right flank of the new German salient and drove it in. It was not the great counterstroke, but the blow which stops a boxer's rush and forces him to pause and consider. Ludendorff realised what it meant, halted, and began to withdraw from the Marne pocket. He had lost the initiative, and had begun his long retreat.

Foch had now freedom of movement, for with him at last were the new American army. In July there were already a million Americans in France. The German command had long been aware of the greatness of this menace, but the German press and people had been told that it was only a force in buckram. Even up to July this newspaper

189

belittlement continued. But at Chateau-Thierry in June an American contingent had fought with furious gallantry ; and on July 15th in the same area one American division and elements from another had rolled back the German assault. These were the troops who, according to the German belief, would not land in Europe unless they could swim like fishes or fly like birds. Like the doubting noble of Samaria, the enemy had declared " If the Lord would make windows in heaven, might this thing be ? " The inconceivable had been brought to pass. Birnam Wood had come to Dunsinane.

On August 8th at Amiens came the true counter-stroke, the first stage of the three months' battle which compelled Germany's surrender. The plan, the choice of the place, and the ordering of the attack were wholly British. Haig had now come to the height of his powers, and was a different man from the cautious, orthodox soldier of earlier days. He had not always been happy with his French colleagues : he was in some ways too like Pétain, and in every way too unlike Foch, to be quite at ease with either of them. But now his mind and Foch's seemed to move towards a closer partnership. The Generalissimo was big enough to take advice, and from Haig he drew not only his chief weapon, the tank, but much of his tactics, and certain vital points in his strategy. The British Army in the past months had suffered far more than the French, but nevertheless they now took the chief rôle, and retained it to the last day of the war. It was Foch's proof of the reverence in which he held his ally.

The Battle of Amiens lasted from August 8th to August 12th, when our advance was halted by the

tangled wastes of the old Somme battle-field. It was
the most brilliantly conceived and perfectly executed
of any British action on the Western Front. Its
success was due to the profound secrecy in which the
forces of attack had been assembled—for example,
the moving from the north of the Canadian corps,
which the enemy regarded as storm-troops, was most
ingeniously concealed ; to the absence of a preliminary artillery bombardment, and the use instead
of a swarm of 456 tanks ; to the ground mist of the
early morning ; to the continuity in the use of
reserves ; and to the wise parsimony which did not
press it too far.

On paper the material gains did not appear
excessive, for, both in ground won and in the number
of prisoners, Germany had often exceeded them.
But it achieved the essential purpose of all fighting,
it struck a deadly blow at the spirit of an already
weakening enemy. Ludendorff has confessed that
" August 8th was the black day of the German army
in the history of the war. . . . It put the decline of
our fighting force beyond all doubt." " We are at
the end of our resources," said the Emperor ; " the
war must be ended." At a conference held at Spa
the Generals informed the Emperor and the Imperial
Chancellor that there was no chance of victory, and
that peace negotiations should be opened as soon as
possible. The most that could be hoped for was an
orderly retirement to the prepared defences of the
Hindenburg Line, a strategic defensive which by its
vigour would win reasonable terms from the Allies.
Ludendorff himself offered his resignation, which was
not accepted. He had lost hope of any gains, and
his one aim was to avoid an abject surrender—not a

promising mood in which to enter upon the most difficult of the operations of war.

Foch was resolved to defeat his hopes, and to hustle him out of all his positions before he could entrench himself, driving the whole vast army back to the narrow gut which led to Germany. But he anticipated at this time a slow advance which would protract the War into the next year. His strategical plan was now in course of revelation. The battle must begin mobile and be kept mobile ; therefore, after striking a blow, he would stay his hand as soon as serious resistance developed. He would not permit himself to become *accroché*, as the British had been on the Somme, at Arras, and at Third Ypres, and as Ludendorff had been before Amiens and on the Lys. But, having stayed his hand, he would attack instantly in another place. Tanks permitted him to mount a new offensive rapidly and frequently, and gave him a means of obviating the clumsiness of the modern military machine. His policy must be a perpetual *arpeggio* along the whole front, which would wear down the enemy's lines and diminish by swift stages his reserves. He would be like a fencer pinking his antagonist, baffling him, wearying him, drawing much blood. There must be no attempt to give a premature *coup de grâce*. Following Napoleon's maxim, he made it his business to keep the battle "nourished" till the moment came for the last stage. He would not press in any section for an ambitious advance or endeavour to force a decision. The campaign must develop organically like a process of nature.

Of this great plan, to which he had contributed, Haig was to be the chief executant. But the British commander, being closer to the actual battle, was beginning to fix a different date for the last act. He was steadily coming to believe that the curtain might fall before Christmas.

II

The temper of Britain through the spring and summer was heavy and apathetic, but now and then it revealed by little spurts of violence how near men and women were living to the outer edge of their nerves. The crisis of March and April had produced a new resolution, but it was a resolution which had no exhilaration in it and little hope. People had begun to doubt if the War would ever end. The night was still so black that they had forgotten that the darkest hour might presage the dawn. The exploit of Sir Roger Keyes at Zeebrugge on St. George's Day woke a momentary thrill, for Britain will always react to a triumph of her Navy. But as the months passed, and the word from the battle-field was only of still further retreats and losses, the popular mind sank again into a dull listlessness.

The news of the turn of the tide in early August did not stir it, for it could not realise its meaning. Everybody was tired and underfed ; the alternation of feverish work and feverish gaiety had unsettled their balance ; an influenza epidemic, too, was each week claiming many hundreds of victims. There was another bout of spy-hunting—a sure proof of frayed nerves. All over the country there were strikes among munition-workers, followed by trouble with the transport services, with the miners, and in August with the London police. These difficulties were solved by the easy method of increasing wages, but sober people began to wonder where this facile business of doles would end. Those in authority, aware that the last stage was approaching, and knowing something of the state of the German people, were anxiously questioning themselves whether a rot might not set in at the very end to nullify all our sacrifice. . . . And then, suddenly, in the autumn the country awoke to the meaning of the news from France. At last we were winning—winning beyond belief. Without excitement, but with a deep half-conscious relief, Britain steadied herself, as a runner steadies himself for the last lap of a race.

Slowly minds began to turn from the preoccupation of the Western Front, and, since we were winning over the whole globe, to realise something of the vastness of the War. It was a task for the imagination, since no man's experience could cover all the many fields. An observer on some altitude in the north, like the Hill of Cassel, on some evening that September, could look east and note the great arc from the dunes at Nieuport to the coalfields at Lens lit with the flashes of guns and the gleam of star-shells. That was a line of fifty miles—far greater than any battle-field in the old wars ; but it was a mere fragment of the whole. Had he moved south to the ridge of Vimy he would have looked on another fifty miles of an intenser strife. South, again, to Bapaume, and he would have marked the wicked glow from Cambrai to the Oise. Still journeying, from some little height between the Oise and the Aisne, he would have scanned the long front which was now creeping round the shattered woods of St. Gobain to where

SURRENDER

Laon sat on its hill. From the mounts about Rheims he might have seen France's battle line among the bleak Champagne downs, and from a point in the Argonne the trenches of the Americans on both sides of the Meuse, running into the dim woody country where the Moselle flowed towards Metz. Past the Gap of Nancy and down the long scarp of the Vosges went the flicker of fire and the murmur of combat, till the French lines stretched into the plain of Alsace and exchanged greetings with sentinels on the Swiss frontier. Such a battle-ground might well have seemed beyond the dream of mortals, and yet it was but a part of the whole.

A celestial intelligence, with sight unlimited by distance, could have looked eastward, and, beyond the tangle of the Alps, witnessed a strange sight. From the Stelvio to the Adriatic ran another front, continuous through glacier-camps and rock-eyries and trenches on the edge of the eternal snows, to the pleasant foothills of the Lombard plain, and thence, by the gravel-beds of the Piave, to the lagoons of Venice. Beyond the Adriatic it ran through the dark hills of Albania, past lakes where the wild fowl wheeled at the unfamiliar sound of guns, beyond the Tcherna and Vardar and Struma valleys to the Ægean shores. It began again, when the Anatolian peninsula was left behind, and curved from the Palestine coast in a great loop north of Jerusalem across Jordan to the hills of Moab. Gazing over the deserts, he would have marked the flicker which told of mortal war passing beyond the ancient valleys of Euphrates and Tigris, up into the wild Persian ranges. And scattered flickers to the north would have led him to the Caspian shores, and beyond them to the table-land running to the Hindu Kush, which was the cradle of all the warring races. Passing north, his eyes would have seen the lights of the Allies from the Pacific coast westward to the Urals and the Volga, and little clusters far away on the shores of the Arctic sea.

The vision of such a celestial spectator, had it been unlimited by time as well as by space, would have embraced still stranger sights. It would have noted the Allied line in the West, stagnant for months, then creeping on imperceptibly as a glacier, then wavering in sections like a curtain in the wind, and at last moving steadily upon Germany. It would have beheld the old Eastern Front, from the Baltic to the Danube, pressing westward, checking and falling back ; breaking in parts, gathering strength, and again advancing ; and at last dying like a lingering sunset into darkness. Behind would have appeared a murderous glow, which was the flame of revolution. Turning to Africa, it would have noted the slow movement of little armies in West and East and South ; handfuls of men creeping in wide circles among the Cameroons jungles till the land was theirs ; converging lines of mounted troopers among the barrens of the German South-west, closing in upon the tin shanties of Windhoek ; troops of all races traversing the mountain glens and dark green forests of German East Africa, till after months and years the enemy had become a batch of exiles. And farther off still, among the isles of the Pacific and on the Chinese coast, it would have seen men toiling under the same lash of war.

Looking seaward, the sight would have been not less marvellous. On every ocean of the world he

would have observed the merchantmen of the Allies
bringing supplies for battle. But in the North
Atlantic, in the Mediterranean, in the Channel and
the North Sea he would have seen uncanny things.
Vessels would disappear as if by magic, and little
warships would hurry about like some fishing fleet
when shoals are moving. The merchantmen would
huddle into flocks, with destroyers like lean dogs at
their sides. He would have seen in the Scottish
firths and among the isles of the Orkneys a mighty
navy waiting, and ships from it scouring the waters
of the North Sea, while inside the defences of
Heligoland lay the decaying monsters of the German
Fleet. And in the air over sea and land would have
been a perpetual going and coming of aircraft like
flies above the pool of war.

The observer, wherever on the globe his eyes were
turned, would have found no area immune from the
struggle. Every factory in Europe and America
hummed by night and day to prepare the materials
of strife. The economics of five continents had been
transformed. The life of the remotest villages had
suffered a strange metamorphosis. Far-away English
hamlets were darkened because of air raids ; little
farms in Touraine, in the Scottish Highlands, in the
Apennines, were untilled because there were no men ;
Armenia had lost half her people ; the folk of North
Syria were dying of famine ; Indian villages and
African tribes had been blotted out by plague ; whole
countries had ceased for the moment to exist, except
as geographical terms. Such were but a few of the
consequences of the kindling of war in a world grown
too expert in destruction, a world where all nations
were part one of another.

III

The advance to victory, like the Somme retreat, cannot be painted on broad lines, for it was composed of a multitude of interlinked actions. The first stage, completed by the first week of September, was the forcing of the enemy back to the Hindenburg Line, an achievement made certain by the breaking by the Canadians on September 2nd of the famous Drocourt-Quéant switch. In the south the Americans under Pershing cut off the St. Mihiel salient, and prepared for their drive northward. The next stage was the breaching of the Hindenburg defences, while Pershing attacked towards Mezières and the Belgians in the north towards Ghent—movements allotted to the last week of September.

It was now the turn of the British War Cabinet to have doubts, and, as it would have put the brake on Allenby in Palestine, so it would have held back Haig. But the British commander had reached the point which great soldiers come to sooner or later, when he could trust his instinct. On September 9th he told Lord Milner that the War would not drag on till next July, as was the view at home, but was on the eve of a decision. He had the supreme moral courage to take upon himself the full responsibility for a step which, if it failed, would blast his repute and lead to dreadful losses, but which, if it succeeded, would in his belief mean the end of the War, and prevent civilization from crumbling through sheer fatigue.

He was justified of his fortitude. On September 26th forty British and two American divisions faced fifty-seven weak German divisions behind the strongest entrenchments in history. By the 29th they had crossed the Canal du Nord and the Scheldt canal, and in a week were through the whole defence system and in open country. By October 8th the last remnants of the Hindenburg zone had disappeared in a cataclysm. Foch's conception had not been fully realised ; Pershing had been set too hard a task and was not far enough forward, when the Hindenburg system gave, to pin the enemy to the trap which had been set. Nevertheless by October 10th Germany had been beaten in a battle which Foch described as a " classic example of the military art." The day of doom was only postponed, and Ludendorff had now no refuge from the storm. Long before his broken divisions could reach the Meuse Germany would be on her knees.

For she was now losing all her allies. They had been the guardians of her flanks and rear, and if they fell she would be defenceless. On September 15th the Allied armies moved forward at Salonika, and within a week Bulgaria's front had collapsed and she sought an armistice. On September 19th Allenby in Palestine opened an action which must remain a perfect instance of how, by surprise and mobility, a decisive victory may be won almost without fighting. This last crusade would have startled the soul of St. Louis and Raymond and Richard of England could they have beheld the amazing army which undertook it. Algerian and Indian Moslems, Arab tribesmen, men of the thousand creeds of Hindustan, African negroes and Jewish battalions were among the liberators of the sacred land of Christendom. Breaking the defence

in the plain of Sharon, Allenby sent his 15,000
cavalry in a wide sweep to cut the enemy's line of
communications and block his retreat, while Feisal
and Lawrence east of Jordan distracted his attention.
The operations moved like clockwork. In two days
the Turkish armies west of Jordan had been destroyed, while that on the east bank was being
shepherded north by the Arabs to its destruction.
By October 1st Damascus was in our hands, Aleppo
surrendered on October 26th, and on the last day
of the month Turkey capitulated. Meantime on the
anniversary of Caporetto Italy had made her last
advance, and the Austrian forces, which had suffered desperately for four years and were now
at the end of their endurance, melted away.
With her gallant army crumbled the country. On
November 4th an armistice was arranged, and at
the same time the Dual Monarchy broke up
into fragments. The Emperor was left alone and
unfriended in the vast echoing corridors of Schön-
brunn.

While Foch continued to play his deadly *arpeggio*
in the West, Germany strove by diplomacy to arrest
the inevitable. Ludendorff stuck to his idea of a
strategical defence to compel better terms, till his
physical health failed and with it his nerve ; but
the civilian statesmen believed that the army was
beyond hope, and that there must be no delay in
making peace. They knew—what the soldiers did
not realise—that the splendid fortitude of the German
people was breaking, disturbed by Allied propaganda
and weakened with suffering. The home front was
dissolving quicker than the battle front. The virus

of revolution, which Germany had fostered in Russia, was stealing into her own veins.

She appealed to President Wilson and attempted to secure peace on the basis of his Fourteen Points, but he very properly replied that the armistice which she sought was a matter for the Allied leaders in the field. From the meeting at Spa on September 29th till the early days of November there was a frenzied effort by German statesmen to win something by negotiations which their armies were incapable of enforcing. But " Time's wingéd chariot " would not wait upon their appeals, for the condition of their land was too desperate. Popular feeling was on the side of Scheidemann's view, " Better a terrible end than terror without end." The American President had curtly informed Germany that, so long as he had to deal with military and monarchical autocrats, he must require " not negotiation but surrender." But the height of the storm is not the moment to recast a constitution, and for the old Germany the only way was not reform but downfall.

No generous mind likes to contemplate the despair of a gallant adversary. By the end of October the German Fleet had mutinied. On the 26th Ludendorff resigned, and the High Command was superseded by the new proselytes of democracy. Everywhere in Germany kings and courts were tumbling down, and various brands of socialists were assuming power. On November 9th the Emperor abdicated and fled to Holland. In the field the German armies were not in retreat but in flight. An armistice had now become a matter of life or death, and on November 6th the German delegates left Berlin to sue for one. Haig and Milner were in favour of moderation in its demands, but Foch was implacable—it must be such as to leave the enemy no power of resistance, and be a pledge both for reparations and security. The delegates had perforce to accept his terms. Very early on the morning of the 11th the document was signed, and it was arranged that on the whole front hostilities should cease at 11 a.m.

It is clear that the Armistice could not have been refused by the Allies, both on grounds of common humanity and in view of the exhaustion of their own troops. It is clear, too, that it was an unconditional surrender, except that it was negotiated before the hands of the fighting men were formally held up in the field. It provided the victors with all that they desired and all that the conquered could give. Its terms meant precisely what they said—so much and no more. Mr. Wilson's Fourteen Points were not a part of them ; the Armistice had no connection with any later peace treaties. It may be argued with justice that the negotiations by the various Governments between October 5th and November 5th involved a declaration of principle by the Allies which they were morally bound to observe in the ultimate settlement. But such a declaration bore no relation to the Armistice. That was an affair between soldiers, a thing sought by Germany under the pressure of dire necessity to avoid the utter destruction of her armed manhood. It would have come about though Mr. Wilson had never indited a single note. In the field since July 15th Germany had lost to the British armies 188,700 prisoners and 2,840 guns ; to the French 139,000 prisoners and 1,880 guns ; to the Americans 44,000 prisoners and

1,421 guns ; to the Belgians 14,500 prisoners and 474 guns. In the field, because she could not do otherwise, she made full and absolute surrender.

In the fog and chill of Monday morning, November 11th, the minutes passed slowly along the front. An occasional shot, an occasional burst of firing, told that peace was not yet. Officers had their watches in their hands, and the troops waited with the same grave composure with which they had fought. At two minutes to eleven, opposite the South African brigade, which represented the eastern-most point reached by the British armies, a German machine-gunner, after firing off a belt without pause, was seen to stand up beside his weapon, take off his helmet, bow, and then walk slowly to the rear. Suddenly, as the watch-hands touched eleven, there came a second of expectant silence, and then a curious rippling sound, which observers far behind the front likened to the noise of a light wind. It was the sound of men cheering from the Vosges to the sea.

IV

Victory dawned upon a world too weary for jubilation, too weary even for comprehension. The crescendo of the final weeks had dazed the mind. The ordinary man could not grasp the magnitude of a war which had dwarfed all earlier contests, and had depleted the world of life to a far greater degree than a century of the old Barbarian invasions. In Britain the figures were too astronomical to have much meaning—nearly ten million men in arms from the Empire, of whom over three million were

wounded, missing or dead ; nearly ten thousand
millions of money spent, and shipping lost to the
extent of seven hundred and fifty millions. The
plain citizen could only realise that he had come,
battered and broken, out of a great peril, and that
his country had not been the least among the winners
of victory. Her fleet had conducted the blockade
which sapped the enemy's strength, and had made
possible the co-operation of Allies separated by
leagues of ocean. Her wealth had borne the main
financial burden of the alliance. Her armies, beginning from small numbers, had grown to be the equal
of any in the world, alike in training, discipline and
leadership. Moreover, her steady resolution had
been a bulwark to all her confederates in the darkest
hours.

He could reflect that such had always been her
record in European wars. At the beginning she is
underrated as a soft and pacific Power already on
the decline. This, in the eighteenth century, was the
view of the continental monarchs ; this, in 1914, was
the view of Germany. She comes slowly to a
decision, enters upon war unwillingly, but wages it
with all her heart, and does not slacken till her
purpose is attained. It had been so in the days of
Philip of Spain, of Louis Quatorze, and of Napoleon.
The "island Poland" ends by finding the future of
the world largely entrusted to her reluctant hands.

It was beginning to dawn, too, upon our people
that they had been fortunate in the leader to whom
their manhood had been entrusted. Haig could
never be a popular hero ; he was too reserved, too
sparing of speech, too fastidious. In the early days
his limitations had been obvious, but slowly men had

come to perceive in him certain qualities which, above all others, the crisis required. He was a master in the art of training troops, and under his guidance had been produced some of the chief tactical developments of the campaign. He had furnished the ways and means for Foch's strategical plans. Certain kinds of great soldier he was not, but he was the type of great soldier most needed for this situation, and he succeeded when a man of more showy endowments would have failed. Drawing comfort from deep springs, he bore in the face of difficulties a gentle and unshakable resolution. Gradually his massive patience and fortitude had impressed themselves on his armies, and after peace his efforts for the men who had fought with him won their deep and abiding affection. The many thousands who, ten years later, awaited in the winter midnight the return of the dead soldier to his own land, showed how strong was his hold upon the hearts of his countrymen.

When Michelet, after the writing of his history, fell ill and rested, he excused himself with the words " *J'ai abattu tant de rois*." Now there was a clattering down of thrones in Europe, and the world was a little dazed with the sound and dust. But to those that endured—in Britain, in Italy and in Belgium— the peoples turned as to the symbol of the liberties for which they had fought. On November 11th great crowds assembled outside Buckingham Palace, moving thither from all quarters by a common impulse, and the King and Queen appeared on the balcony to receive such an acclamation as has rarely greeted the sovereigns of an unemotional people. The next days were full of pregnant ceremonial. On

the 12th they went in solemn procession to St. Paul's
to return thanks to the Giver of victory. In the
following week they drove through the east and south
and north districts of London, and paid a brief visit
to Scotland. On the 27th the King visited France.
He had been on the battle-field three months before
during the great advance of August 8th, and now
he could examine at leisure the ground where victory
had been won, and greet his troops as they moved
eastward to the German frontier. In Paris, at
banquets at the Elysée and the Hôtel de Ville, he
spoke words of gratitude and friendship to the French
people.

On Tuesday, November 19th, in the Royal Gallery
of the Palace of Westminster, he replied to the
addresses of the two Houses of Parliament. There,
in the presence of political leaders, and the great
officers of State, and representatives of India and of
all the Britains overseas, he expounded in simple
words the debt of the nation to its fleets and armies
for their achievement ; the pride of Britain in her
Allies ; the unspectacular toil of the millions at
home who had made victory possible, and the task
still before the nation if a better world was to be
built out of the wreckage of the old.

In what spirit shall we approach these great problems ?
How shall we seek to achieve the victories of peace ? Can we
do better than remember the lessons which the years of war have
taught, and retain the spirit which they have instilled ? In
these years Britain and her traditions have come to mean more
to us than they had ever meant before. It became a privilege
to serve her in whatever way we could ; and we were all drawn
by the sacredness of the cause into a comradeship which fired our
zeal and nerved our efforts. This is the spirit we must try to
preserve. It is on the sense of brotherhood and mutual good
will, on a common devotion to the common interests of the

nation as a whole, that its future prosperity and strength must be built up. The sacrifices made, the sufferings endured, the memory of the heroes who have died that Britain may live, ought surely to ennoble our thoughts and attune our hearts to a higher sense of individual and national duty, and to a fuller realisation of what the English-speaking race, dwelling upon the shores of all the oceans, may yet accomplish for mankind. For centuries Britain has led the world along the path of ordered freedom. Leadership may still be hers among the peoples who are seeking to follow that path. God grant to their efforts such wisdom and perseverance as shall ensure stability for the days to come.

It was an expansion of the words which he had spoken eight years earlier in the month before his Coronation, a homily upon Milton's proud saying : " Let not England forget her precedence of teaching the nations how to live." He was entitled so to exhort his people, for he and his house had played their part manfully in the struggle, unostentatiously performing hard and monotonous duties, sharing gladly in every national burden. The country knew this and turned to the King as to its best friend, with something warmer than respect, profounder than loyalty. A year before there had been an attempt in Germany to drum up monarchical sentiment by films and lectures and articles showing the simplicity and devotion of the Imperial household. There was no need of such artifices in Britain, for royalism was the willing creed of all. Its most impressive manifestation was not the crowds around Buckingham Palace, or the splendid occasion in the Royal Gallery, but what happened on the late afternoon of Armistice Day. In the wet November dusk the King and Queen drove in a simple open carriage through the city of London, almost unattended and wholly unheralded. The merrymakers left their own occupations to cheer, and crowds accompanied the carriage through the new-lighted streets, running beside it and shouting friendly greetings. It was an incident which interpreted better than any formula the meaning of a People's King.

PART III

CHAPTER I

SOUR-APPLE HARVEST

I

A WAR solves no problem but the one—which side is the stronger. In November 1918 a menace had been defeated and a great arrogance overthrown. These gains were indubitable, but what then? It is an old assumption that some spiritual profit is assured by material loss and bodily suffering; but it is certain that the moral disorder is at least as conspicuous as the moral gain. One bequest of war is an impulse to lawlessness. The passions of many millions cannot be stirred for years without leaving a hideous legacy. Human life has been shorn of its sacredness, death and misery and torture have become too familiar, the old decorums and sanctions have lost something of their power. The crust of civilisation has worn thin, and beneath can be heard the muttering of the primordial fires. Again, with the suspension of a great effort, there is apt to come a debauch of theorising. Principles, which seemed fundamental, are a little weakened, and men are inclined to question the cardinal articles of their faith. The world becomes one vast laboratory, where ignorance clamours for blind experiments with unknown chemicals.

But the chief consequence of so great a war

as this was mental and moral fatigue. Minds
were relaxed and surfeited, when they were not
disillusioned. They had had enough of the heroic.
After the strain of the distant vision they were apt
to seek the immediate advantage ; after so much
altruism they asked leave to attend to private interests ;
after their unremitting labours they claimed the right
of apathy. The conundrums of peace had to be
faced not only by jaded statesmen, but by listless,
confused peoples. Listless, but also restless ; Mr.
Lloyd George found the right word for the malady
when he described it as a " fever of anæmia."

The situation was the more dangerous for the
Allies, because the intricate business of peace should
have been the work of the peoples, as they had been
the architects of victory. The War was not won by
the genius of the few but by the faithfulness of the
many. It had been a vindication of the essential
greatness of our common nature. The problem now
was colossal, for, if many ramshackle structures had
been demolished, the ground was heavily cumbered
with rubble, and there were sharp differences of view
as to the edifice to be built. But the peoples seemed
to stand aside, and cast the whole burden of settlement on statesmen whose shoulders were already
weary. Nothing was more striking than the popular
apathy about the business of peacemaking. The
statesmen, too, had no great dominant mind and
character among them. The world was like Rome
after the murder of Cæsar, like America after the
death of Lincoln. History will pay respectful tribute
to the able and tenacious men thrown up by the years
of war, but it is doubtful if many names will live in
the popular memory. Perhaps only the fantastic

figures whose doings were like those of the heroes of fairy tales : Lenin, the dark Ogre ; D'Annunzio, the glittering Knight-Errant ; Colonel Lawrence, the eternal Younger Son.

Britain caught the same infection as the rest of the world. The prevailing mood after peace was one of satiety with high endeavour, the mood of the Restoration after Cromwell's discipline. The bow had been stretched too tight and must relax. After toil there must be a play-time. Older men turned to the job of settling themselves again. For long they had been living on sufferance, with the feeling that in a night all they possessed might vanish ; now they suddenly felt secure, and clung passionately to what remained of an ordered life. There was a good deal of irrational optimism about. As for youth, it shut its ears for a little to every call but the piping of pleasure. There was a general loosening of screws and a rise in temperature. The War was a memory to be buried. Young men back from the trenches tried to make up for the four years of natural amusement of which they had been cheated ; girls, starved for years of their rights, came from dull war-work and shadowed schoolrooms determined to win back something. Perhaps the gaieties of the first months of peace had for their god Dionysus rather than Apollo, but the reaction from gravity was inevitable and not unwholesome.

> Tiny pleasures occupy the place
> Of glories and of duties : as the feet
> Of fabled fairies, when the sun goes down,
> Trip o'er the grass where wrestlers strove by day.

For the Government there could be no turning aside to leisure. They had an urgent task in front

213

of them and problems to solve where mistakes might mean anarchy or revolution. Inevitably they did not grasp the full meaning of the situation. They thought of their task as rather to restore a damaged old world than to grapple with something novel and undefined ; they assumed, too, that the same vitality which had carried the nation through war would not be wanting in peace. But they had the wisdom to see that peace would not follow naturally on victory ; that it was in itself a construction, a slow and difficult attempt to bridge a gap. Their aim was to maintain the same corporate national effort as had been successful in war.

The purpose did them credit, but it was shallowly interpreted, and it led to the blunder of the 1918 General Election. Statesmen, who had criticised the soldiers harshly for their blindness, were now in their own province to be not less myopic. The instinct which led to the election was right, but its conduct was disastrous. It was desired to obtain a fresh mandate from the nation for the work of peace-making and to continue the coalition of all parties ; both worthy aims, if they had resulted in brigading behind statesmen the wisest and sanest patriotism of the country. But for sitting members the test of patriotism was a solitary division in the House of Commons in the preceding May on a criticism of the Government by a distinguished staff-officer—a criticism which may have been ill-timed, but was assuredly not factious or unfair. The docile were given " coupons," the malcontents were outlawed. The immediate consequence was a descent from the Prime Minister's high words after the Armistice about a peace based on righteousness, and the need of putting away " base,

sordid, squalid ideas of vengeance and of avarice."
The coupon candidates swept the board, and gave
the Government a huge working majority with 484
members ; Labour returned 59 strong, and the non-
coalition Liberals were reduced to little more than
a score. But the mischief lay less in the result than
in the conduct of the election campaign. Responsible
statesmen lent themselves to cries about " hanging
the Kaiser " and extracting from Germany impossible
indemnities. Britain stood before the world as the
exponent of the shoddiest of false patriotisms instead
of the reasoned generosity which was the true temper
of the nation.

The result was one of the least representative
Parliaments in our history. A batch of leaderless
trade unionists constituted the official Opposition ;
the rest was, in Mr. Lloyd George's words, like a
chamber of commerce. It did not represent the
intelligence of Britain, since it was mainly an
assembly of well-to-do mediocrities ; it did not represent the better side of the national temper ; it left
out certain vital elements of opinion, which were in
consequence driven underground. It mirrored the
nation in its worst mood, and it did much to perpetuate
that mood. The feverish vulgarities of the election
created impatience in many classes, in returning
soldiers, in munition-workers, in the circles of labour,
which made infinitely harder the business of resettlement. It gravely weakened the prestige of Parliament, which had been largely in abeyance during
the War, and which could not afford any decline in
dignity at a time when many minds were turning
away from constitutionalism. Above all it impaired
the authority of Britain in the coming peace councils.

She alone could exercise a moderating and healing influence, both from the authority which the War had given her, and from her detachment from old European jealousies. But the Prime Minister would go to these councils bound by extravagant election pledges ; and whatever words of conciliation he might speak would be obscured by ugly echoes of the blatancies of the polls.

II

The history of the Peace Conference in Paris, which filled the early months of 1919, has been written in detail in many volumes. Its work has been bitterly criticised, and on it have been blamed most of the later misfortunes of Europe. But it is probable that our successors will take a friendlier view, and will recognise more fully the difficulties under which it laboured and the many valuable results which it achieved. Its position was very different from that of the Congress of Vienna in 1814. Then the victors held most of Europe and had armies ready and willing to carry out their commands : now they were so weary that the further use of force was almost unthinkable. Then a little group of grandees, akin in temper, met in dignified seclusion. Now a multitude of plenipotentiaries sat almost in public, surrounded by hordes of secretaries and journalists, and under the arc-lamp of suspicious popular opinion. The difference in the complexity and scale of the two inquiries is shown by the resulting treaties. The 120 articles of the Treaty of Vienna were signed by seventeen delegates ; the Treaty of Versailles contained 441 articles and seventy signatures. The business was indeed so vast that the mechanism was constantly changing. At first the main work was in the hands of a Council of Ten, representing the five great Powers ; then it fell to the American President and the European Prime Ministers ; at the end the dictators were Mr. Wilson, M. Clemenceau and Mr. Lloyd George.

Had these three architects of destiny been fully agreed, or had they been men of a different stamp, things might have gone better. But all three were leaders of democracies, and they had to take many things into consideration besides the merits of the case. M. Clemenceau was the intense nationalist. Policy to him meant the security of France, and he translated every world problem into the terms of an immediate and narrowly conceived national interest. Mr. Lloyd George, subtler and more far-seeing, took broad views, but his power was weakened in his colleagues' eyes by the election he had fought and the intransigent following which it had given him. From Mr. Wilson, who had lived apart from the actual conflict, there might have been expected a cool and dispassionate mind, as well as a unique authority. But he found himself on unfamiliar ground, and his political mistakes in his own country had made it doubtful whether America would ratify his con-clusions. His idealism, it soon appeared, was the the voice of one crying in the wilderness, and not the creed of a great people. His self-confidence made him cast himself for too high a part, and he failed to play it ; in the end his decline in health forced him into aloof and impotent criticism. The framers of the Treaty of Vienna a century before were fortunate in that they were simpler men, whose assurance was better based, and who were happily detached from popular passions. " There are times when the finest intelligence in the world is less serviceable than the sound common sense of a *grand seigneur*."*

The three main subjects were territorial adjustments, reparations, and the provision of machinery to ensure peace. Under the first the map of Europe was redrawn, and some parts of the map of the world. The Conference, it should be remembered, did not start with a clean slate ; the Austrian Empire had already gone to pieces, and Poland had come automatically into being. A number of treaties, of Versailles, of St. Germains, of Trianon, of Neuilly, of Sèvres, laid down the new boundaries, and mandates dealing with territory taken from enemy states were settled later by Allied Ministers sitting as a Supreme Council. Germany had her borders trimmed, but she was not dismembered. France claimed the Rhine as her frontier, but was given instead a limited occupation of the Rhineland, supplemented by a joint military guarantee by Britain and the United States, which was dropped since the latter Power declined to ratify.

As for the rest of Europe, there was a juggling with border lines and populations which, since it was done in haste, could not be wholly satisfactory. The ill-omened concept " self-determination " hag-rode the Conference, and was enforced on occasions where there was no serious self to determine. Historic states were split into fragments, for which there could be no hopeful future. The upshot was that in Europe, instead of twenty-one sovereign states, there were now twenty-six, each with all the appurtenances

* F. S. Oliver, *The Endless Adventure* : III, 109.

of exclusive statehood. The danger was obvious, but at least it could be said that the arrangement was broadly in accordance with the popular will. Mr. Churchill has calculated that now not three per cent. of the European peoples " are living under Governments whose nationality they repudiate."

The penal proposals which had played so great a part in the British election, were reduced more or less to the matter of reparations. The disarmament of Germany was strictly enforced, but it was combined with a solemn pledge by the other nations themselves to disarm, which promised trouble in the future. It was resolved that the defeated Powers should pay the whole cost of the War, which in effect meant Germany, since the others were bankrupt. No victor has ever succeeded in reimbursing himself for his losses, and a strange blindness seemed on this point to have overtaken the public mind. Germany was rich indeed in capital wealth, but it could not be conveyed to her creditors, and her exportable surplus had never been great, and was now likely to be small. She could only pay large sums by borrowing from one or other of the Allies. Yet a committee of solemn pundits in Britain had fixed her capacity to pay at the preposterous figure of 24,000 millions. The Conference reduced this sum to less than half, and during subsequent years it was whittled down to 6,000 millions, to 2,000 millions, and in 1932 further payments were dropped. More unfortunate still was the clause which extorted from Germany a confession of her sole responsibility for the War. It was not the business of any conference to anticipate the judgment of history, and to force a proud nation to confess that her sacrifice had been a crime was a breach of the human decencies.

The treaty with Germany was signed at Versailles on June 28th, the anniversary of the Serajevo murders. The place was the Hall of Mirrors, where nearly half a century before the German Empire had been founded on the degradation of France. For those whom history had taught to distrust reapportionments of territory and experiments with nationalities, the hopeful element lay in its prefix—the Covenant of a new League of Nations, the one remnant left of Mr. Wilson's dreams. Once again the world sought to bind itself by words to follow its better nature, and wistfully hoped that the reaction against the horrors of war might result in an abiding determination for peace.

A machinery was provided to give system to this desire. Membership of the new League was open to any self-governing State which accepted its principles ; it required of its members to refrain from war until the quarrel had been submitted to its judgment, and to take corporate action against any breaker of the peace. It was not a super-state with a military force as its sanction, but a league of states whose effectiveness in a crisis would depend upon how far its members were prepared to act collectively. There was no abandonment of sovereign rights, except in a minute degree. It was to begin with to be a league of the victorious and the neutral Powers, but the defeated Powers were given the right of later entry. From the start it was handicapped by the facts that it was widely regarded as the caretaker of the Peace treaties and therefore suspect by those who found them irksome, and that America refused to join, thereby weakening any chance of collective action. But it was the best that could be got at the moment in the way of international co-operation, and even its meagre provisions were soon proved to be in advance of the general opinion of the world.

III

For a moment, but only for a moment, after the signing of the treaties, there was a sense of peace and stability. Then everywhere in the world came un-settlement and confusion, economic or political or both, save where beyond the Atlantic the United States sat bland and impregnable. Wise men had prophesied that the liquidation of the War would take a generation to complete, and that a further sacrifice would be required of many remnants of the old regime. The sixteen years since Versailles fall in the retrospect into three divisions. For some five years there was chaos in many lands and un-certainty in all. Then there seemed to come a time when men everywhere drew breath, and found that they had at any rate put together a makeshift shelter. But the liquidation had been retarded, not com-pleted, and at the end of the second quinquennium came an economic collapse which shook even America's foundations. It was a time which saw not only the death of old things but the birth of violent novelties. After a forest fire, when the great trees have gone, new seedlings spring up, and mysteriously they are often of a different species from the growths that have been destroyed.

Britain, desperately busied with setting her house

in order, was compelled to lend a hand in straightening out the world's tangle. Foreign politics were once again a vital interest to her, as they had been in the days of Palmerston and Gladstone. No one of her domestic problems but had affiliations with the ends of the earth. On the peace and prosperity of the globe depended her export trade, her vast system of overseas lending, her position as a financial centre, her hope of building up a new and better society and thereby winning something from the sacrifice of war ; and the interest of her Empire was not less vitally engaged. The background to any picture of post-War Britain must therefore be the vast shifting kaleidoscope of the world.

It may be questioned whether history can show a fortitude superior to that of the German race, soldiers and civilians alike, during the four years of war. Germany was at her last gasp before she surrendered. Surrender did not break the tough spirit of her people. They crushed a communist attempt to follow the Russian model, and produced, while they were starving and bewildered, some semblance of a national Government. They received the hard conditions of Versailles with protests but with dignity. And then they set themselves against desperate odds to build up their broken dwelling.

They had first to fight the spectre of famine. The blockade was continued into 1919, and it was only the protests of the British soldiers on the Rhine that forced the Allies to attend to their duty of provisioning a starving land. As it was, a huge proportion of her people, the children especially, were suffering from under-nourishment. There was an extreme shortage of raw material, and she had neither the money to purchase it abroad nor the shipping to import it. Her highly developed system of agriculture was in ruins. She was saddled with an enormous and undetermined debt. For four years she had lived under a military discipline ; that had disappeared, and the new republic had to improvise a new social and governmental framework ; there were a thousand elements in her society which threatened anarchy, while Russia at her door was waiting to fire the tinder of revolution. The fragments left of the Dual Monarchy were in no better case. Austria was reduced to a great city and a small surrounding enclave which could never be a true economic unit. Hungary, also bankrupt, was sullen, perplexed and impotent.

General Smuts signed the Versailles Treaty only on the ground that something of the kind, however imperfect, was needed before the real work of peacemaking could begin. But the Treaty was to prove a grave hindrance in that task. The key-point was Germany, for Austria and Hungary were incapable of independent action and had to be nursed back to life by the League of Nations. The German people on the whole remained loyal to their bourgeois republic. Wounded pride made sporadic nationalist risings inevitable, and a certain Austrian mason, Adolf Hitler by name, took a hand in the Munich troubles, and was sent to prison. The German Government could only maintain itself against communist and nationalist opponents by a continuing protest against the impossible severity of the reparations clauses of the Treaty. To the disarmament provisions they docilely submitted. The problem of the next few years was how to square what France regarded as her rights and her necessities with the hard facts of the case.

For France the War had ended in anxiety and disappointment. Germany had been defeated, but that defeat had not been her doing ; without the help of Britain and America she knew that she would have been beaten to the ground. The glory, which was the due of her heroism, was revealed as tarnished and unsubstantial. With a population of forty millions she had to live side by side with a population of sixty or seventy millions, who were not likely to forget Versailles. She was in the position of a house-holder who has surprisingly knocked out a far more powerful burglar, and it was her aim to see that her assailant was not allowed to recover freedom of action. Therefore her policy, of which M. Poincaré was the chief exponent, must be to keep Germany crippled and weak, and to surround her with hostile alliances. The terms of the Treaty, both as to reparations and disarmament, must be interpreted according to the strict letter. No one can deny that her fears were natural. It is easy for those who live high above a river to deprecate the nervousness of one whose house is on the flood level.

To Britain it seemed that, with every sympathy for French anxiety, it was impossible to keep a great Power in perpetual tutelage, and that the only hope for France, as for the world, lay in establishing a new international system which would give political security and economic co-operation to all its parts. Mr. Lloyd George, while he remained in office, strove honourably for this end, and his policy was maintained by his successors. Conference followed

conference, each accomplishing something, but not
the whole. The amount of reparations was fixed,
reduced, and again reduced. But meantime
Germany's finances were going from bad to worse,
and France chose to take her own way, moving,
under M. Poincaré's direction, further and further
from Britain. She distrained on her debtor's assets
by occupying in January 1923 the Ruhr area, which
was Germany's chief source of coal and pig-iron,
in order to obtain what she called " productive
guarantees." The experiment was not a success, for
it was met by a vigorous passive resistance, and after
nine months she withdrew her troops. But the
mischief had been done, a fatal blow had been struck
at the infant republic, and the German mark went
out of existence. Then Britain intervened, and
appealed for the co-operation of America ; and a
Committee, presided over by General Dawes, laid
down a new scheme of reparations, based " on
business, not politics . . . the recovery of debt, not
the imposition of penalties."

For a little there was a rest from friction. The
massive figure of Hindenburg as President gave
dignity to the republic, and the German Government
under Stresemann set itself to fulfil the Versailles
terms, and to make friends with its neighbours. The
Locarno treaties of 1925, under which Britain and
Italy guaranteed her western frontier, seemed to
bring Germany again into the family of Europe.
In 1929 the Dawes Plan was superseded by the
Young Plan, and for a little there was hope that
Stresemann's policy, continued by Brüning, would
lead her on the path of international co-operation and
a moderate constitutionalism. But the mischief had

gone too deep. The ruin of the mark had destroyed the middle classes ; youth found itself without opportunity ; a proud people knew itself to be defenceless while its neighbours had not disarmed. Inspired by the Munich mason a great wave of nationalism surged through the land, a nationalism combined with much revolutionary social doctrine. If Germany were not given her rights she would take them by force and defy the world.

Parliamentary government fell to pieces. Hitler became Chancellor in 1933, and proceeded to crush opposition by the familiar methods of the dictator. On Hindenburg's death he became also President, and summoned his country to a new and austerer discipline. The League of Nations was powerless ; short of declaring war, France could do nothing ; Germany was again outside the European comity, speaking wild words and brandishing a broken sword. But Hitler had given his country, and especially its youth, a new hope. A spirit had arisen, arrogant, boastful, intolerant, which was at any rate more promising than a flaccid passivity. Germany was once again in the melting-pot, and another country was added to the roll of those which had discarded democracy.

For the fashion of dictatorships was spreading. It looked as if in critical times a people needed some intense concentration, and that this was the simplest method for those who had not, like Britain, a long tradition of self-government behind them. Austria had abandoned parliamentaryism ; so for a time had Greece and Spain ; Hungary had never had it. Russia had become half tyranny and half theocracy.

SOUR-APPLE HARVEST

For a year after peace Britain continued the policy, which was justified in the concluding stages of war, of assisting Russian armies which were attempting to break the Bolshevik power. There may have been something to be said for the plan of turning the still-embodied war strength of the Allies, and perhaps of Germany, against the Moscow regime to blot out a monstrosity—it would certainly have saved many million Russian lives ; but there was small justification for supporting limply anti-Red armies which could not conquer. Our intervention only consolidated the Bolshevik power. Russia had few friends in Europe except among the dervishes of her own creed, since she preached war and practised intrigue against the whole of Western civilisation. But, after an invasion of Poland which was repelled with French help, she settled within her natural bounds, and by the end of 1920 the new regime was more or less established.

Lenin was a realist in his fanaticism, and modified the strict letter of communism in his New Economic Plan to permit of a certain amount of private property. He died in the beginning of 1924, but his policy endured, and the communist purists were gradually replaced by more practical visionaries, notably by the Georgian peasant Stalin, whose ruthless sagacity served his country well. The new regime had now been recognised by most of the Powers, and to-day the United States completes the roll. Gigantic efforts were made by successive economic plans to increase production, and remarkable advances were achieved in certain public services. Russia, with apathy among most classes but with a fiery enthusiasm among the young, was docile under the most

227

exacting paternalism that the world has known, with the mummified Lenin in his tomb in the Red Square as the fetich-god of a land which had rejected all other deities. It was ruled by a junta, and ultimately by the will of one man.

Different in spirit but alike in kind were the governments in Italy and Turkey. In Italy the parliamentary system had no deep roots, and after the war it became little better than a farce. The land was weary and disappointed ; her Prime Minister had left the Versailles Conference in disgust, and her nationalists complained with some reason that she had been given the scantiest rewards for her sufferings. Had there been a leader she might have followed the path of Russia, but the communists who during 1920 seized factories and brawled in every industrial area had no plan of action. A young ex-socialist journalist of thirty-seven, Benito Mussolini, who had been wounded in the campaign, set himself to combat this aimless revolution. He organised a confederation of ex-service men, and smote anarchy wherever he found it, taking for his badge the *fasces* of the old Roman magistrates, and adopting the black shirts of the Italian storm-troops in the War. His creed was nationalism and royalism, combined with drastic industrial reforms. In October 1922 he led his followers to Rome, the Government fell, and a Fascist Cabinet was formed. He then set himself to reorganise the social and administrative life of the country, and in four years had Italy quiet under his hand.

Parliamentary government in the common sense was abolished, and in its place rose the corporative state, in which capitalism was permitted, but controlled.

All classes were integrated in a great national effort, in which rights and duties were scrupulously balanced. The system involved a dictator at the head, for there must be a final authority to supervise the intricate machine ; it involved, too, the disappearance of free speech and a free press, since such personal activities interfered with the smooth competence of the whole. Mussolini achieved astonishing results ; he suppressed disorder and enforced efficiency ; he brought the Vatican again into touch with the national life ; he restored confidence to a dispirited nation. He did not seek to make Italy, like Russia, an enclave for a fantastic experiment, but showed himself anxious to play his part in the communal life of Europe. He faced the many economic difficulties with courage and resource, and gave his land all the appurtenances of civilisation except individual liberty.

The case of Turkey was somewhat different, and her ascent to a self-conscious nationalism was the chief of post-War romances. In November 1918 she had seemed of all the enemy Powers to be the most thoroughly beaten and broken, and to lie helpless in the hands of the Allies. But the Turk was not dead, and he found his saviour in an Anatolian soldier, Mustapha Kemal, who had won fame at Gallipoli. The ill-inspired invitation to Greece, for which Britain was mainly responsible, to occupy the Smyrna area kindled the embers of Turkish patriotism. Kemal fell upon the Greeks and drove them into the sea ; he led his armies to the Dardanelles, where a clash with British troops was only averted by the wisdom of the British commander ;

at Lausanne he obtained a wholesale revision of the Treaty of Sèvres.

Then he set himself to rebuild his country on the strong foundation of the Anatolian peasantry. He smashed the old unity of Islam and abolished the Caliphate, but he gave Turkey, the nation, a unity which she had never known before. She was now a republic under Kemal as dictator, and his first task was to secularise her, and, in a year or two, to clear away most remnants of traditionalism. Women were emancipated from their former bondage, education was revolutionised, the whole machine of finance and industry was recast. Kemal was not merely a domestic reformer ; like Mussolini, he showed himself a wise international statesman. He made friends with Greece, exercised a soothing influence in the Balkans, intrigued no more with Russia but turned his eyes westward, and in 1932 brought his country into the League of Nations. There are few precedents in history for such a national resurrection.

IV

In fifteen years the prophets had been discomfited. So far from building up again—with differences— the old regime on the old principles which had been assumed to be elemental truths, all of Europe, save France and Britain, had struck camp and set out to discover new habitations. The War had been fought by the peoples rather than by leaders ; now the leaders had emerged and the peoples put their fate into their hands. New monarchies had arisen on the ruins of the old, more arbitrary and absolute, and names like Führer and Duce and Ghazi carried a weightier spell than those of emperor and king. Never had personalities mattered so much, for Stalin was Russia ; Mussolini, Italy ; Kemal, Turkey ; and Hitler, Germany. Democracy, which the War seemed to have glorified, was largely in ruins. Russia and Turkey had cut adrift from their pasts, but Italy sought to dignify her new creation by linking it to the glories of ancient Rome, and Germany had evolved a most unhistorical theory of an old Nordic culture to which she was returning. This last dream had an ominous connotation. For it may be read in Tacitus how into the sombre grove of the High God of the Teutons none might enter save with a chain round his neck, to show his subjection to the divinity. The old legend is a parable ; those gods were tyrants, and their mandate was to enslave. A hundred years before Heine had prophesied that some day the Gods of the North would rise from their graves to the troubling of Europe.

This flight from democracy, this satiety with freedom, had been accelerated by the War, but it was not its product, for it had been long a-coming. Perhaps democracy had been too absolutely defined. Its principles had been treated as universal truths for all peoples at all times, when they could only be made to work under certain conditions. The mystical view of the State as an " end in itself," which must override the individual life, had been emphasised by the discipline of the War, but it was no new thing in the world. Mankind is always prone to deify the work of its hands, and to make a god of the authority it chooses, whether it be Holy Church,

231

or Holy King, or Holy People. The reaction which might have been looked for after peace was nullified by the continued unsettlement of the world. Men were unwilling or unable to stand alone ; they huddled into hordes for safety and warmth, and were glad to surrender their wills to whoever or whatever promised security. The ordinary citizen had lost that confidence in himself which is the only basis for democracy.

This instinct to crowd together might at first sight appear to offer some hope for a union of nations. But unfortunately the new internal integration of peoples was apt to be on a narrow chauvinist basis ; the refuge they sought must be isolated, exclusive, a Border keep bristling with defences, and not an open law-abiding city to which all were welcome. During the fifteen years from its foundation the League of Nations passed through many vicissitudes. It did admirable work on the less controversial international questions, and it proved a godsend to the relics of the Dual Monarchy. But it was heavily handicapped by the absence of America, and by the withdrawal from it in later years of important States. Its machinery proved to be faulty, and too many of its members were half-hearted. When its authority was challenged, as at Corfu and in Manchukuo, it had no sanctions with which to enforce it. It did many good things, but the work was not spectacular and won it little prestige. The hubbub of conflicting nationalisms drowned its still, small voice of reason.

One of its major tasks was disarmament. The question was debated at many conferences, but was invariably blocked by national fears and jealousies and technical difficulties. In this matter the record of Britain was blameless, for she was not only the most vigorous supporter of a general disarmament, but she had herself disarmed beyond any other Power. The Kellogg Pact of 1928, which excluded war as a " legitimate instrument of policy," could be no more than a declaration of pious opinion in the absence of a specific machinery to enforce it. More hopeful at the time seemed the Washington Conference of 1921, which limited the naval construction of Great Britain, the United States, Japan, France and Italy. This line was followed in numerous arbitration arrangements, and in regional and group pacts such as the Locarno treaties. These at any rate narrowed the possibilities of conflict, though to the peace universalist they seemed a dangerous return to the old system of alliances.

The comparative failure of internationalism was not due to the insensitiveness of any country to the cataclysmic effects of another war. The popular horror was deep-grained ; indeed it is doubtful if at any time since the Armistice it would have been possible to mobilise any European nation for war without a certainty of revolution. Mr. Churchill's solemn words were the general faith.

Manhood, . . . without having improved appreciably in virtue or enjoying wiser guidance, has got into its hands for the first time the tools by which it can unfailingly accomplish its own extermination. That is the point in human destinies to which the glories and toils of men have at last led them. They would do well to pause and ponder upon their new responsibilities. Death stands at attention, obedient, expectant, ready to serve, ready to shear away the peoples *en masse* ; ready, if called

233

on, to pulverise, without hope of repair, what is left of civilisation. He awaits only the word of command. He awaits it from a frail, bewildered being, long his victim, now—for one occasion only—his Master.

The difficulty lay in the vicious circle into which the debates inevitably moved. Fear produced armaments ; that fear could only be allayed by a system of collective insurance with the proper sanctions ; such a system involved interference with sovereign rights, which most States were not prepared to accept. Fear, a very real fear, was not strong enough to conquer national pride, a pride intensified by the movement towards new national disciplines and integrations. The most needful restoration of a people's confidence quickened that people's pride and lessened its fear. The true spirit of peace-making had not yet been generated, and the words of Bernard of Marlaix haunted many minds :

Pax erit omnibus unica, sed quibus ? Immaculatis,
Pectore mitibus, ordine stantibus, ore sacratis.

In such a flux of things Britain had a dual task. She had to interest herself in the difficulties of other nations, as a world-wide Empire which could not afford to be indifferent to any change in any part of the globe, as a principal belligerent and therefore a principal architect of peace, and as the one Power in the Old World which still stood firmly in the ancient ways. But with these heavy preoccupations she had also the duty of revising her own policy, which had suffered the full blast of the winds blowing from the outer spaces. Except for one brief moment after peace she caught no blink of the sun. For fifteen years she had to struggle in the mire of that dismal thaw which is the certain consequence of war.

CHAPTER II

THE CHANGING EMPIRE

THE first British Empire ended with the loss of the American colonies, the second with the first shots of 1914. During the political interregnum of the War the third slowly came into being. Lord Rosebery in a famous passage has spoken of the Empire " growing as trees grow while men sleep," but the phrase is only half the truth. The progress of any great and enduring thing is largely unconscious and secret, like the growth of a plant or the changes of the seasons. But in the making of the Empire there have been times when problems have had to be faced and solved, and steps of high importance voluntarily and consciously undertaken.

The War was such a season. In it the Empire may fairly be said to have come of age, and become an alliance of adult nations. It was a unit in 1914, as a unit it entered upon war, and as a unit it made peace ; but its assistance in the field was wholly voluntary, its war effort spontaneous and not dictated. During those four years autonomy acquired a new meaning, for to the right of deciding on policy was added the willing acceptance of executive duties. Dominion prime ministers sat in London with British representatives as an Imperial War Cabinet. The Dominions as national entities signed the treaties of peace. The old dream of Imperial Federation had

236

faded out of the air. The new circumstances required a more elastic constitution.

The overseas territory taken from Germany enlarged the area of certain of the Dominions and widely extended the direct responsibilities of Britain. The Dominions were members of the League of Nations from which the mandated authority sprang. For good or for ill they had been brought into the orbit of international affairs, and must have an international outlook of their own. At the same time their kinship with the Mother Country and with each other had become a closer thing, after four years of common sacrifice. The economic difficulties of the post-War world were felt by them scarcely less acutely than by Europe. They realised their common interest with Britain, and, as the political bonds slackened and disappeared, there was a general instinct that new ones must be fashioned, the ties of a working alliance which would enable the Empire in practical matters to speak and act together.

The King was King of Britain, but also Emperor of India, and Sovereign of all the Britains overseas. The Throne was the one binding link that survived. During the controversies that followed it remained, except in one case, the cherished centre of unity, around which union could grow. As such its value was beyond price, for it provided a steadfast foundation on which a new working mechanism could be constructed and a new theory of Empire developed.

I

The first problem was Ireland. Ever since the spirit of Elizabethan and Cromwellian intolerance began to die at the close of the eighteenth century the British people had been under two delusions. They imagined that Ireland was a country which had, though in an imperfect form, the same traditions and antecedents as Britain, and that the Irish were only backward cousins of their own. The profound differences of race and history were innocently forgotten. It is possible that in 1886 a chance was given us to make Ireland a part of the United Kingdom in something more than name, for there are moments in history when a bold act may seal up the past and swing a nation's development into a new orbit. Be that as it may, the chance was not taken. The old sores festered, the old hostilities remained, and the unsettlement of the immediate pre-War world, her unfortunate position in British party politics, and a revival of interest in her native culture, fostered in Ireland, especially among her youth, a spirit which would be content with nothing short of national independence. This spirit was the more formidable since it disregarded the former methods of controversy and set to work to devise a new technique.

The solemnity of war might have turned the unrest into other channels, but official pedantry checked at birth the growth of a new sentiment. The consequence was that, while many thousands of Irishmen were fighting in the armies of the Empire, several bodies in Ireland were preparing on their own account for a different kind of war. The Easter Rising of 1916 revealed these hidden fires. That pitiful and heroic attempt of young idealists to enforce a creed, which was dearer to them than life, exasperated Britain, who could not understand why Ireland should try to weaken her hand in a war which was fought not for Britain but for civilisation, and who did not realise how alien the Irish vision was from her own. It was easily suppressed, but the aftermath was tragic ; the barbarities were not all on one side, and the Government dabbled alternately in mercy and in severity. The result was an immense strengthening of Sinn Fein and Irish republicanism. Various later efforts at conciliation were fruitless, and the proposal to apply conscription in the spring of 1918 did not help matters. There remained little of the Irish character as Bede had drawn it twelve hundred years before, " a harmless people most friendly to the English."*

Peace came, but not to Ireland. In the election of November 1918 the old Nationalist leaders had gone, and the old Nationalist party disappeared. Sinn Fein won most of the Irish seats, and in January 1919 set up a parliament of its own in Dublin and proclaimed an Irish Republic. Mr. Eamon de Valera, who had escaped from an English jail, became its President, its supporters armed, and the King's writ ceased to run in Ireland. In 1920 a new version of the Home Rule Bill was passed, setting up parliaments in Dublin and Belfast. Ulster accepted the scheme, but South Ireland scornfully rejected it. From now on the issue was war, war between the levies of the Republic on the one side, and on the other the police, enlarged by the " Black and Tan " auxiliaries, and a part of the British army.

It was war, but, since it could not be conducted by the normal etiquette of war, it was also a reign of terror. In the first half of 1921 there were two

* " Gentem innoxiam et nationi Anglorum semper amicissimam."—*Hist. Eccles.*, iv, 26.

governments in Ireland, and between these mill-stones were ground what Sir Henry Wilson used to call the " decent, quiet, peaceable people." It was a grim and hideous time, for both forces were out of hand, and the spectacle was presented to the world of a great and civilised Power sanctioning reprisals in kind for the atrocities of banditti. Ministers were in an intolerable dilemma. They must either use their military strength to stamp out a rebellion of British citizens at Britain's door, or they must admit that this was no rebellion, but a war of principles, and treat with the enemy. In the then temper of Britain and her Government the latter course meant a heavy sacrifice of pride.

The impasse was ended by the King. Now, as ever, it was the duty of the Throne to unravel the tangle into which people and Government had drifted. On June 22nd, 1921, the Parliament of Northern Ireland having come into being in accordance with the act of the previous year, the King, in Belfast, made one of the most notable speeches of his life :

I could not have allowed myself to give Ireland by deputy alone my earnest prayers and good wishes in the new era which opens with this ceremony, and I have therefore come in person, as the Head of the Empire, to inaugurate this Parliament on Irish soil. . . .

The eyes of the whole Empire are on Ireland to-day—that Empire in which so many nations and races have come together in spite of ancient feuds, and in which new nations have come to birth within the lifetime of the youngest in this hall.   I am emboldened by that thought to look beyond the sorrow and the anxiety which have clouded of late my vision of Irish affairs. I speak from a full heart when I pray that my coming to Ireland to-day may prove to be the first step towards an end of strife amongst her people, whatever their race or creed.   In that hope I appeal to all Irishmen to pause, to stretch out the hand of forbearance and conciliation, to forgive and to forget, and to join in making for the land which they love a new era of peace, contentment and goodwill. It is my earnest desire that in Southern Ireland, too, there may ere long take place a parallel to what is now passing in this hall, that there a similar occasion may present itself and a similar ceremony be performed.

For this the Parliament of the United Kingdom has in the fullest manner provided the power ; for this the Parliament of Ulster is pointing the way. The future lies in the hands of my Irish people themselves. May this historic gathering be the prelude of a day in which the Irish people, North and South, under one Parliament or two, as these Parliaments may themselves decide, shall work together in common love for Ireland upon the sure foundation of mutual justice and respect.

Such an appeal could not be disregarded. The Government, who had been gradually moving towards some scheme of Dominion home rule such as Mr. Asquith had long advocated, opened negotiations with the Irish leaders. The latter were now tending to divide into two camps ; the realists, like Arthur Griffith and Michael Collins, who wanted the substance of independence and were not inclined to quibble about forms ; and the symbolists—the word is used in no contemptuous sense, for symbols are precious and potent things—who sought not Dominion status but independence with all the paraphernalia of independence, and to whom the oath of allegiance and the headship of the King were badges of servitude. It was a tragic irony that the stumbling-block should be the Sovereign who was the most earnest advocate of peace. The Conference in London lasted till December 6th, when a treaty was signed under which the Irish Free State came into being, with the status more or less of a self-governing Dominion. The result was a triumph for the diplomatic finesse of Mr. Lloyd George ; it was a triumph of character, too, for the Conservative statesmen, like

Lord Birkenhead and Sir Austen Chamberlain, who imperilled their careers, and for the Irish delegates, who imperilled their lives.

The Irish Parliament, Dail Eireann, passed the Treaty by a small majority, but Mr. de Valera and the austerer republicans went into opposition. He was not willing to accept the oath of allegiance ; he held that Dominion status was unworthy of a nation which was an ancient kingdom and itself a mother country ; his dream was of Ireland as a separate Power, not within the Empire, but externally allied to it for defence and foreign affairs. On this narrow margin the land was plunged for a year in civil war. It is the fashion of revolutions to devour their offspring, and Ireland's was true to type. That unhappy country has been apt to discard or destroy her best. Arthur Griffith indeed died in his bed : but Michael Collins and, later, Kevin O'Higgins perished by violence ; Sir Henry Wilson, always an Irishman first, was the victim of assassins on the doorstep of his London house ; and Erskine Childers, than whom no revolution ever produced a nobler or purer spirit, was shot by the order of the new Irish Government. Mr. William Cosgrave, who succeeded Griffith as President, slowly broke the republican opposition till Mr. de Valera, defeated but unconverted, called off hostilities. Then for ten years he laboured to restore his country and patch up the economic fabric, and incidentally gave it once again a worthy part in imperial and international councils. The nations since the War have had two kinds of leaders : the rhapsodists who inflame and embolden, and the plain, homely realists who try to heal. In the latter class Mr. Cosgrave has had few superiors.

THE CHANGING EMPIRE

But Ireland had not found peace. The symbolists were still powerful, and their appeal was especially to uprooted and malcontent youth. In February 1932 Mr. Cosgrave was defeated in a general election in which his opponents offered no bribes except the chance of sacrifice and the certainty of conflict. Mr. de Valera had the mind of some great ecclesiastic of the Middle Ages, half mathematical, half mystical, and to him the symbol was dearer than the fact. He had never accepted the Treaty, and he set himself to whittle it away. He plunged his country into a tariff war with Britain over his refusal to pay the land purchase instalments, and pointedly disregarded all the formalities which membership of the Empire involved. Since Ireland could not repudiate the obligations of such membership and at the same time receive its benefits, she became in fact an alien to the Commonwealth. So the miserable position came about that Britain was forced to stand on legal points which had little bearing on the true case, and to do much to kill by economic policy those elements in Irish life which made for stability and progress.

Many have wished that the Treaty and its heritage of debate could be blotted out and the cards dealt afresh, for the present situation does justice neither to Britain's dignity nor to her generosity, and it inflicts futile suffering on Ireland. The obstacle to a fresh deal is not Britain's pride, but Britain's apathy about the whole business. Once Ireland meant something to us, but now she means little. We alternately scolded and petted her, which was a proof of interest, even if the interest was chiefly in a political counter ; now there is no British election in which her name is mentioned. The horrors of 1921, of which we naturally heard more of one side than of the other, inspired wrath, which presently, after our fashion, changed to boredom. We had had enough of Ireland ; let her stew in her own juice and permit us to attend to our own affairs. Yet this very popular apathy might make it easier for statesmanship to break the vicious circle, for the present situation offers no hope for the future. Grattan's words of Ireland still remain true : " The Channel forbids union ; the Ocean forbids separation."

II

The other imperial problems of those years concerned Egypt, and India, that empire within the Empire. In the War the former became perforce a British protectorate, and peace saw the rise of a violent nationalist agitation, encouraged by the ill-omened Allied doctrine of " self-determination." Britain, busied with many tasks, postponed any settlement and deported Zaghlul, the nationalist leader ; widespread rioting followed, until Lord Allenby restored a semblance of order. Then a little tardily the British Government sent out a mission under Lord Milner to report on the future government of the country. The mission, boycotted by the nationalists, advised that Egypt's independence should be recognised, but it was not till nearly two years later that Britain finally declared Egypt a sovereign state, with certain reservations concerning defence, foreign affairs, imperial communications, and the Sudan. This by no means satisfied the extremists, rioting and assassinations were resumed, and an exasperated British Cabinet was forced to strong measures. Egyptian troops were withdrawn from the Sudan, the embryo parliamentary constitution was suspended, and presently the Sultan Fuad and his Ministers took over the government as a virtual autocracy. The situation was now much the same as under the Cromer regime, except that Egypt had not the benefit of a great Englishman and a band of competent and incorruptible British administrators. The ancient land of the Nile has not yet found a self to determine. More fortunate has been the fate of the two mandated states, Palestine and Iraq. The second, after twelve years within the Empire, during which it cost Britain much money and much diplomatic and military effort, has now attained to independent statehood and membership of the League of Nations. Palestine, where Britain in face of many difficulties has laboured to carry out her pledge to create a Jewish national home, is at the moment one of the few prosperous states in the world.

In India much history has been made since the King spoke at Delhi in 1911. The war served to hasten the growth of those national aspirations which had been whetted by the Minto reforms. In 1917 the Secretary of State for India, Mr. E. S. Montagu, made a momentous declaration in the House of Commons :

The policy of His Majesty's Government, with which the Government of India are in complete accord, is that of the increasing association of Indians in every branch of the administration, and the gradual development of self-governing institutions with a view to the progressive realisation of responsible government in India as an integral part of the British Empire.

These cautious but pregnant words were followed in 1919 by the Montagu-Chelmsford reforms, which

245

in the Provinces divided the functions of Government into two classes, some reserved exclusively for the Governor and his Council, and some entrusted to Ministers responsible to the new local Legislatures. A Central Legislature was also established, consisting of two Houses, with important legislative powers, but with the right left to the Viceroy to override its decisions. The plan was to be revised within ten years. It was formally inaugurated at Delhi, in February 1921, by the Duke of Connaught on behalf of the King-Emperor.

The new system had a disastrous birth. There was grave trouble on the Afghan frontier, and in India itself; it was boycotted by the National Congress, and Mr. Gandhi, the prophet of a kind of mystical reaction, preached a crusade of pacific non-co-operation. Yet the complex, hybrid system worked better than might have been supposed, and it was at any rate an education for many Indians in the rudiments of parliamentaryism. But revision was not only desirable but a statutory duty, and in 1927 a commission under Sir John Simon went out to India to study the problem. The Simon report, the ablest state paper of recent years, proposed full responsibility for the Provinces, but not for the Central Government, unless and until the Ruling Princes should enter the system, which might then be on a federal basis.

There followed a series of Round-Table conferences and peripatetic commissions to work out the details of the new constitution. The fact that the Princes were willing to come in met the Simon conditions, and it became possible to envisage a federal constitution with a large measure of responsibility at the

Centre. The Government plan was embodied in a White Paper ; this was submitted to an inter-parliamentary committee, which, after sitting for eighteen months, published its report in the late autumn of 1934. It accepted the main principles of the White Paper scheme, which indeed were not only the logical and inevitable conclusions of the Montagu declaration of 1917, but a rational deduction from the changed conditions of the East and the new temper of India and of the world.

Lord Minto, a plain country gentleman and no politician, was fond of saying that the objection to governing a country against the will of its inhabitants was not moral but physical ; it was simply impossible ; the wildest tyranny must be at least acquiesced in or it would not last a day. To govern 350 millions by force is not feasible, even if we wished it ; some co-operation by the people is necessary since politics in India are fast spreading from the classes to the masses. Criticism of the details of the British policy is inevitable, for it is beyond question a long step forward into shadowy places. Yet there is general agreement on the need for some such stride and on its direction. The Empire was not won, and it has not been maintained, by standing stiffly in the old ways, but by repeated bold experiments. That instinct, which has guided us in the past, is to-day more vital than ever, since the events of the last twenty years have been like a compounding of chemicals in which no elements have been left unchanged. Every question requires a fresh analysis. Many principles, once held to be ultimate verities, have been revised, and the whole range of methods. In the realm of economics this is universally admitted, and it is not less necessary in the constitutional sphere.

Two further reflections may be added. It has been argued with truth that political systems do not appear out of the void, but have their roots deep in history, and depend for their success upon the nature of the society to which they are applied. Parliamentary democracy is not a thing which comes into being full grown ; it has a slow genesis and requires long preparation ; a form of government which has served well in the West cannot be indiscriminately applied to the East ; western civilisation has behind it the Renaissance, the Reformation, and the French Revolution, and India has none of these things. The answer is that the British scheme differs organically from any western constitution. What is proposed is not a blind transference to alien conditions of a highly idiomatic kind of government, but an attempt to build upon the facts of modern India a special and appropriate type of polity.

Lastly, it is said with some truth that parliamentary democracy has lost caste in Europe. Why, it is asked, should we be ready to saddle India with a discredited type of government ? The answer is that happily it is not discredited in Britain or in the British Empire. We are the honourable slaves of our own achievements. For a century we have been labouring to inspire India with our political philosophy, and we have largely succeeded. We have welcomed her as an organic part of an Empire which is based on that philosophy. We have helped to create in her habits of thought of which that philosophy is the natural outcome. We cannot exclude her from sharing in what we regard as our best.

THE CHANGING EMPIRE

Meanwhile the self-governing part of the Empire was engaged in working out in practical detail the new imperial doctrine which at the close of the War had won general acceptance. In former days the handling of foreign policy had been in the hands of the British Cabinet, and its decisions had bound the Dominions. Under its auspices treaties had been signed, and by its will war had been declared and peace concluded. But the new conception of an alliance of sovereign States made this procedure impossible. A Dominion could not pledge itself to war except with the consent of its own Parliament ; it must have the right to make treaties in the name of the King ; it must, if it so desired, have diplomatic representation in foreign capitals. The problem was how to combine these necessary functions with some unifying principle which would enable the Empire to have a continuous foreign policy, and in a crisis to speak to the world with a single voice.

When Mustapha Kemal's troops advanced to the Dardanelles in the autumn of 1922 and for a moment Britain seemed to be on the verge of war, Mr. Lloyd George appealed to the Empire for aid. The response of the Dominions, half-hearted or resentful, was a warning that the old methods had gone for ever. The ensuing Treaty of Lausanne was formally accepted by Canada, but not any obligations arising from it, and at the Imperial Conference that year it was resolved that " no treaty should be negotiated by any Government of the Empire without due consideration of the possible effects in other parts of the

Empire." That year, too, Canada arranged a fishery treaty with the United States, the signature of which she insisted must be by a Canadian plenipotentiary under powers issued to him by the King. From 1924 onward various Dominions appointed their separate diplomatic representatives. In the Locarno treaties the Dominions and India were excluded from the British obligations arising thereunder, unless they specifically assumed them.

The Empire was drifting into a constitutional tangle which it was the business of the Imperial Conference in 1926 to unravel. A formula drafted by Lord Balfour, attempted a definition of the relations of Great Britain and the Dominions :

> They are autonomous communities within the British Empire, equal in status, in no way subordinate one to another in any aspect of their domestic or external affairs, though united by a common allegiance to the Crown, and freely associated as members of the British Commonwealth of Nations.

From this certain consequences followed, of which the chief was that the British Government, as Government, had no right of interference in Dominion affairs, and that a Governor-General must represent the King and the King alone, and be appointed on Dominion advice. A committee of lawyers and officials sat in 1929 to work out certain conclusions, and the result was the Statute of Westminster, which became law in 1931. This enactment removed, with a few small exceptions, every shackle from a Dominion's sovereign power. It left the Crown as the sole legal link holding the alliance together, and it provided, therefore, that any law affecting the Crown should require the assent of every Parliament in the Empire. If the scriptural *Via, Veritas, Vita* be taken as a

motto for any great human undertaking, the two
last words have been for the Empire interpreted and
fulfilled. From the days of the Elizabethans it has
had the Life. It has now by slow stages reached
the Truth, a doctrine which permits free growth
within a generous framework. It remains to find
the Way, the machinery of an executive alliance, the
means of giving expression to its unity of spirit.
These means we are still in process of discovering in
the various departments of economics, foreign affairs
and defence. The conference at Ottawa in 1932
was such an attempt ; so were the numerous trade
arrangements negotiated in the last few years. The
pressure of economic problems is forcing the com-
ponent parts of the Empire into a closer collaboration, and correcting the fissiparous tendency which
was inevitable after the dissolution of the older bonds.

A court of law, I think, would have some difficulty
in interpreting the exact meaning of the Balfour
Definition, or in pronouncing upon the full implica-
tions of the Statute of Westminster. Can a Dominion
remain at peace if Britain is at war ? In theory,
perhaps, but scarcely in fact, for no imperial statute
would prevent Britain's opponent from bombarding
the Dominion's ports if it so desired. A Dominion
may have the power to secede from the Empire, but
what then becomes of its relation to the Crown ?
What is the right of the constituent provinces of a
Dominion against a Dominion Government, rights
of which Britain in some cases remains the trustee.
What indeed is the true meaning of a Dominion ?
We have left unexplored certain *arcana imperii* in the
hope that the need for exploration may never arise.
That has always been the British way. When we

start to write out a constitution we never make a complete job of it. We do not believe that the meaning of an Empire, which is in continuous growth, can be enshrined in any document. So instead of a definition we have been content with spacious generalities.

But one thing has emerged from the debate, the tremendous meaning of the Crown. It is the foundation of the new doctrine, the one principle which gives unity to a vast growth whose destiny is unpredictable. Without it no tie of sentiment or blood or tradition would bind for long. To the Empire it provides a centre for its long memories and a personality for its devotion. There can be no question but that it has acquired since the War a far deeper and more intimate meaning for the Britains overseas. The journeys of the Prince of Wales, and his power of charming every class, have brought the royal life into the kindliest contact with their own. When on Christmas Day in recent years the King has spoken to all his people, his wave-length has been subtly attuned to their hearts. He is not Sovereign or symbol, but the Head of the Family, who summons his household round the hearth, and commends it to " the Father of Whom every family in heaven or on earth is named."

CHAPTER III

A HOUSE IN ORDER

I

HUMAN nature loves to dignify the past and decry the present. The new is disturbing, or at the best drab ; to look back to a golden age is one means of acquiring hope for the future, since what has once been may come again. The earliest Babylonian tablet is a lament for the decay of the age, and every epoch which seems brilliant to our retrospect had its prophets of doom. There were doleful critics in the time of the Antonines, and the peace of the Middle Ages seemed chaos to those who lived under it ; the Elizabethans had their pessimists ; Wordsworth thought the times degenerate during which Trafalgar was won and Napoleon conquered ; and the rock-like serenity of the Victorians appeared to contemporaries a flimsy and febrile thing. The British people have always made a speciality of a kind of self-abasement which depreciates themselves and exalts their ancestors. In every decade we have had honest men and sincere thinkers, the burden of whose plaint has been *Troja fuit*.

After peace we had a full chorus of such croakers. In the first confusion of resettlement the pre-War years, which had once appeared so comfortless, seemed an unbelievable paradise of ease. The heroism and discipline of the War were regarded as a supreme effort, in the making of which Britain had exhausted herself. We had to face unparalleled problems with wearied brains and slack sinews ; the best of our youth lay dead on the battle-fields, and the elderly and the old had to bend their shoulders to tasks for which they were not fit. The decline of Britain seemed to many a foregone conclusion. But, as Adam Smith on his death-bed told a doubting friend, there is a good deal of ruin in a country. I question if the historian will find in Britain's record a more honourable page than that which tells of the decade and a half after peace. Without the frosts of war to nerve her or the sun of prosperity to warm her, she trudged most gallantly along the muddy roads of the great thaw. With broken tools she built the rudiments of a new dwelling which, if the fates are kind, may be a worthier edifice than that which it has replaced.

The main concern for Britain, as for other nations, was economic—how to keep body and soul together. In its preoccupation with material needs all the world had gone Marxist. The problem was how to pass from the unbridled extravagance of the War to a normal life. We had been living on stimulants, and we must somehow transfer ourselves from dope to diet. There was a brief gleam of prosperity just after peace, when the replacement of stocks required still further expenditure, and then the nation settled itself to a long thankless toil in the shadows. The first tasks were extraordinarily difficult. The huge armies had to be somehow fitted into civil life. A swollen officialdom had to be drastically purged. Industries had to be freed from Government props and made to stand alone. House-room had to be found for hundreds of thousands who were houseless ; the price of living must be brought down ; wages, too, must be reduced from war-time extravagance to some scale on which they could continue. It soon became apparent that the War, whatever it may have done for men spiritually, had left a hideous material mess to be cleaned up.

The first duty was to cease spending more than we could afford ; no easy thing, for our obligatory expenses were almost beyond our earnings. We had to face some eight thousand millions of war debt, and this meant a scale of taxation which crippled industry and bore crushingly on all but profiteers. There was a strenuous effort after economy in administration, and presently some fifty millions were lopped off the civil estimates, but a formidable difficulty remained. We had created a great system of social services, which the well-being of the nation required should be en-larged instead of diminished. They involved high taxation, and that, and our wage level, greatly in-creased the cost of production. But while our costs had risen our business was declining. We had lost our industrial pre-eminence in the world's markets, since other nations had climbed, or were climbing, to our level. Our exports, visible and invisible, looked like soon ceasing to pay for our necessary im-ports. The whole nineteenth century fabric of British trade was breaking down. With shrinking markets, and the cost of government, local and central, nearly three times what it had been in 1913, with taxation absorbing one-third of the nation's income instead of one-eighth, we were ceasing to be able to pay our way. The industrial worker was already receiving a higher remuneration than was warranted by the sale-value of his product.

The situation was met by a vigorous effort on the part of industry both to enlarge its house and to set it in order. Agriculture, which had for a little during the War taken its old place in the nation, was allowed to slip back into a melancholy trough, but industry in the face of the gravest difficulties put its shoulder stoutly to the wheel. There was a second industrial revolution, under which a variety of new businesses arose, chiefly luxury products, and much of the green landscape of southern England became hideous with raw factories. The War, too, had stimulated research, and in many forms of production there was a notable technical advance. But, while this improved the efficiency of the machine, it dispensed with part of the human factor, and by increasing unemployment increased industry's overhead burdens. To add to our other difficulties there was the growing economic nationalism of much of the world, an infection which had not yet seized on Britain, so that the industrialist, heavily taxed, and encumbered with high costs, had to compete abroad in lands hedged round by tariffs, and at home against foreign imports, cheaply produced and often subsidised.

Under such handicaps the marvel was that our industrial system did not crumble altogether. It had another drawback to contend with, for at the start the national policy was a banker's policy. Deflation was the watchword, and the international stability of money was regarded as the key to trade revival. In April 1925 the Chancellor of the Exchequer, Mr. Churchill, took the fateful step of returning to the gold standard at the pre-War parity.

This was deflation with a vengeance, for the amount of money was curtailed, and therefore internal prices dropped while interest charges and wages were un-reduced. This added to the cost of production at home, while the price of British goods to the foreigner was automatically increased. It was orthodox finance in the old sense, and it re-established Britain as the world's financial centre, but it crippled still further our export trade, and prepared the way for wage troubles in our exporting industries.

Seven difficult years ensued. Other Governments followed the British return to gold, but at something far below the pre-War parity. Meantime unemployment grew, and it became clear that some of our heavy industries had sunk permanently to a lower level. Money, the medium of trade, was losing its old, stable flexibility. Under the futile system of war debts and reparations a large part of the world's capital was diverted into barren channels. The debtor countries could not pay their debts in goods, since their creditors had erected colossal tariff walls, and the consequence was that their exports were diverted to Britain, the one great free-trade area that remained. But the payment received for these goods did not go to buy British produce, but to purchase gold wherewith to satisfy their creditors. Gold, instead of being a running and fertilising river, had become a frozen glacier bringing death in its train.

In these years the country sorely required some other heartening than the obligatory optimism of statesmen. As in the War, the King did much by his constant visits to distressed areas and to em-barrassed cities to keep the popular temper steady. His words were always of hope, a reminder that

257

Britain had passed through dark places before and yet had emerged into the sunlight. Take, as one instance out of many, what he said at Glasgow in 1931, when he opened a new dock on the Clyde :

What chiefly impresses me is your present courage and enterprise. At a moment of industrial depression you are steadfastly preparing for the long-hoped-for trade revival. I believe that those who have faith in the future of our nation will not be disappointed, and will reap the full reward of their foresight.

Two centuries ago Glasgow was the pioneer in the development of trade with North America. That enterprise, in the words of the best-known Glasgow citizen in literature, Bailie Nicol Jarvie, was the most fortunate event in her history, " since St. Mungo first caught herrings in the Clyde." Moreover, it was the first step which raised Scotland from a poor and backward country to a foremost place in all human activities. She has been the window from which Scotland especially has looked out upon the world. She has been the port from which Scotsmen have gone forth to colonise and develop new lands. For a century her ships have sailed every ocean, and there are few corners in the world, however remote, where you cannot find a Glasgow engineer.

It is a great record, but I am convinced that it is not yet ended. There are still new worlds for Glasgow to conquer. . . . The motto of this great city is " Let Glasgow flourish." When Scotsmen aspire earnestly to a purpose, the purpose is already half accomplished. We shall watch with cordial interest the fulfilment of that hope.

Disaster was imminent, for the whole mechanism of the world's commerce was out of gear. The climax began in the autumn of 1929 with the downfall of America's swollen prosperity. Like the first break-up of the ice in a river, cracks started in all quarters, and then came a slow loosening and upheaving. Future historians will have no doubt as many explanations of the cause of the great depression as of the origin of the War, but certain facts are indubitable. The money system of the world was no longer adequate to the complexities of the world's trade, complexities increased by political troubles, by economic nationalism, by the unbalanced position of gold, and by a distrustful and uncertain popular temper. Increased production could not be brought into relation to increased demand.

In Britain the crisis came in the summer of 1931, when a Labour Government was in power, a Government in which only a few were able to read the signs of the times. The warnings of Mr. Snowden, the Chancellor of the Exchequer, had little effect upon some of his colleagues, whose financial creed was a blend of mysticism and emotion. A creeping sickness was spreading over the world, and during the summer the symptoms became acute, first in Austria, then in Germany, and last in Britain. A conference of European Ministers in London in July provided no remedy. On the last day of the month the May Report was published, which revealed that, on the present basis of income and expenditure, there would next year be a deficit in the British budget of over 120 millions. There followed at once a heavy withdrawal of foreign balances, and the Bank of England had to seek assistance from France and the United States. On August 24th the Labour Cabinet resigned, and the King invited the Prime Minister to form an emergency Government of all parties. In September a supplementary Budget was passed by the House of Commons, which by heavy economies and increased taxes provided a small surplus for this and the coming financial year.

The emergency Cabinet was formed to keep Britain on gold. It found the thing impossible. On

Monday, September 21st, we left the gold standard, an example speedily followed by a number of other nations. Next month Ministers went to the country as a National Government, and were returned to power by an immense majority. Their task was to restore the international credit of Britain by scrupulously balanced budgets and by a reasonable reduction of the adverse balance of trade. The gold standard proved to have been largely a bogy; it had seemed the only palladium when we were on it, but we found that we did very well without it. The sterling group soon became a force in the world. There was no fall in the purchasing value of the pound at home, and its depreciation in terms of certain foreign currencies was in effect a bonus to our export trade. We had redressed the inequalities of our 1925 ambitions.

The years since 1931 have seen Britain, by a great effort of sacrifice and discipline, restored not only to an economic, but to a moral, leadership among the nations, and her Dominions have walked in the same path. She has eschewed flashy panaceas and perilous short cuts, and stuck to the highroad of common sense. Difficult problems still confront her, but more than any other Power she has attained poise, confidence, and a measure of stability. The ill weather continues, but to meet it she has strengthened her house walls. . . . But it is a new house. The year 1931 marked the end of the Victorian regime which had given her prosperity. Changed conditions have forced her to accept some degree of economic nationalism, and free-trade in the old sense has departed. The corporate effort of the War has had its effect, and the nation has been ready to use more amply, when circumstances warranted it, the powers of the community. Capital is more under State control, because it has often to seek the help of the State. We are beginning to realise that the machine, if wisely used, may play the part which the slave system played in ancient Athens, and provide an ampler leisure for the citizen. Yet the phrase, the " new socialism," is a misnomer. Collectivist methods are used, not because they are deduced from any creed, but because they happen to meet the case. In accordance with her secular practice, Britain has troubled very little about political theory ; she accepts change under the potent compulsion of facts.

II

To all this upturning of foundations Labour could not be insensitive. At the end of the War it was in a difficult mood, conscious of its power, shaken out of many of its old beliefs, uncertain of its future. The example of Russia was disquieting, for, though the older and wiser saw the tyranny under the veneer of that workers' dictatorship, younger men were excited by the spectacle of a dream come true in a night. To such, evolution seemed a refuge for the feeble, and revolution the method for the strong. Yet in the labour unrest there was very little that was doctrinaire. Nationalisation was demanded not so much as an advance towards state socialism as on the practical ground that private ownership meant local inequalities, and—with the war mobilisation of industry in mind—inefficiency ; and a short working day because more men could be employed. But the

261

cardinal point was higher wages, to meet the rise in prices, and to give the worker the margin above subsistence which is the basis of freedom.

In the first two years of peace there was a big crop of trade disputes, inevitable in the dislocation of economic life. Three great unions, the Miners, the Railwaymen, and the Transport Workers, formed a Triple Alliance. Through the early months of 1919 a Coal Commission sat on the miners' problem, and from its somewhat confused findings there emerged a shortening of hours and an increase in wages. That summer and autumn there was serious trouble with the railwaymen. In April 1920 the Triple Alliance threatened a general strike in support of the miners' case, a strike which was only called off at the eleventh hour. The following year there was another stoppage in the coal industry, but the other members of the Triple Alliance held their hand, and the miners had to fight their battle alone. The trouble in that industry was not merely a dispute between men and masters, but the fact that in the new conditions of the world it simply could not maintain its old scale of employment. Subsidies from the Government tided it over from year to year, but it was becoming plain that the flash-point was not far distant. In 1925 another Coal Commission was appointed which rejected nationalisation, but proposed new wage scales and other reforms on a national basis. The miners refused the terms, the Government subsidy ceased on April 20th, 1926, and on May Day the General Council of the Trade Union Congress decreed a general strike.

The General Strike—it was not general, for only certain key industries were affected, and it was not quite a strike—marked the end of an epoch in our industrial life. Labour had come to believe that it could dictate to the nation, and it found that the nation was its master. The Government, which had striven for peace until the last moment, used its statutory emergency powers, and worked on a plan which it had elaborately prepared. Food supplies were perfectly organised, a reduced system of transport was provided, and order was strictly maintained. The amateur proved that at a shift he could do the work of the expert. Youth rose to the crisis as it had risen to the call to war, and the universities emptied themselves into the dock, railway, and bus services. There was no violence, and everywhere there was good temper and a determined geniality. To the outside world it was an amazing exhibition of coolness and common sense. The trade union leaders, who had released the jinn from the bottle without considering the consequences, were alarmed and bewildered. They realised that the feeling of the nation was against them, and that their action might make their funds liable at law for colossal damages. Almost at once they sued for peace, and after nine days they called off the strike. The miners struggled on alone till November, when they too capitulated, having driven a good many more nails into their industry's coffin.

The events of May 1926 did much to clear the air and purge the mind of Labour of certain post-War delusions. The unions had challenged the nation—innocently but unequivocally—and had found the nation by far the stronger. There was another wholesome result. All classes had served together in the trenches, and a very solid respect had grown up in each for the quality of the others. But the post-War youth had had no such opportunity, and the notion had spread in Labour circles that the young men of the middle and upper classes had not the same spirit and hardihood as themselves. On this point the General Strike left no doubt, and the foolish truculence which had characterised the previous years was sensibly abated.

It was well that this should be so, for the Labour party was now the second greatest of the political camps of Britain. Though its professed creed was socialism, it had little in common with the socialist parties of the Continent. Its backbone was the trade unions, which were the most English thing in England. They were more radical than socialist, and in a sense more conservative than radical. Their object was not to pull up things by the roots, but to get their own roots deeper. Their faults lay in an occasional blindness of eye and confusion of head, not in any unsoundness of temper or heart. Their attempts at dictatorship were bungled tactics, not a serious strategy. But, while they formed the strength of the Labour party, from their sectional narrowness of outlook they were also its weakness. They brought to the House of Commons a refreshing realism, for they spoke as experts on many practical things, and their stalwart vernacular was a joy amid the clipped conventions of parliamentary speech. But larger questions they were apt to judge on too low a plane and with imperfect knowledge. The corrective was to be looked for in the socialist intellectuals, of whom they were inclined to be suspicious, but who applied to policy a wider education and broader sympathies. These were often viewy and pedantic, but as a group they were serious students of public affairs, with a genuine scientific apparatus behind them. It was well for Labour, and well for the country, to have this laboratory of experiment and thought.

The conditions of working-class life had on the whole been greatly improved since the War. Higher wages did not lead to waste, but to higher standards of decency and comfort. The average household had better food, better clothing, more margin for amusements, wider horizons. Small wonder that they struggled to maintain what they had won. That was for those in employment : for the unemployed, who had now passed beyond the two million figure, there was a bare subsistence and a tragic idleness, a steady loss of their technical skill, and a slow souring and dulling of mind. Yet in the very tragedy there were elements of hope. A problem of such magnitude required for its solution not only the energies of the State but the thought and the good-will of every private citizen ; and, largely owing to the work of the Prince of Wales, these were forth-coming. People began to recognise a personal duty. Also there was a stimulus to clearer thinking and to an effort to remake our whole industrial machine. Hitherto the task had been to remedy the defects of industrialism, now it was to transform industrialism itself. One social danger was however forgotten— the embarrassed middle-classes, especially their youth. When a young man of that class was unemployed, he was the care of nobody ; when he was employed, it was too often on a job without light or horizon. From such natural discontent fascism, or some other authoritarian creed, might draw many recruits.

Had some Rip van Winkle gone to sleep on the eve of the War, and awakened any time in the first decade of peace to cast an eye over our society, he would have been first impressed, I think, by the superficial levelling up of classes. Men and women could no longer be judged by their clothes. These had become simpler and more uniform. A clerk was as well dressed, and in much the same way, as a Guards officer, and a village girl as the lady of the manor. People—the women especially—would have appeared to him slimmer and more vital. He would have missed the old stately ritual of London life. The capital now looked more like a provincial city, for the top-hat had largely gone, club life was a declining thing, the great mansions had become blocks of flats, and the " season," shorn of its old splendours, now lasted most of the year. He would have been struck by the trimness and the healthier appearance of youth. Parliament, perhaps, would have seemed to him rather a shabby assembly. In the country he would have found towns spreading into mushroom suburbs, and ancient villages blotched with bungalows. He would have been amazed at the size and populousness of the roads, and the scarcity of horses. Famous houses which he had known were now either pulled down or turned into schools and asylums, the parks had been ploughed up and built upon, and their owners had migrated to suburban or continental lodgings with a few family heirlooms and the war-medals of their dead. But he would have found village life gayer and freer, if less idiomatic. He would have noted, too, that the hunt meets were as large as ever, and that a new gentry had made its appearance. As after the Wars of the

Roses a small squirearchy was growing up on the ruin of the grandees ; and he would have consoled himself by reflecting that it was the new modest manors which had produced some of the greatest Elizabethans.

As he looked more closely into things our Rip van Winkle would have been awed by the widespread passion for entertainment. He remembered that Disraeli more than half a century before had told Lord Rowton that the true revolution would come in Britain when the bourgeoisie took to amusing itself. Games bulked larger than ever in the nation's eyes. The cinema had become a universal habit ; twenty millions visited it each week. There were now seven million wireless sets, the remotest hamlets were forests of wireless poles, and daily about half the population was entertained and instructed from the air. Instructed !—that was what impressed him. The demand for a greater margin of leisure involved the means of filling that leisure, and almost every form of entertainment had its educative side. There would soon be no more pleasant oases of unsophistication. The workers and the peasants were getting to know how their neighbours lived and how the world lived. Knowledge was being diffused in the widest commonalty, shallow perhaps, but still knowledge. A mighty transformation was in progress, managed by the people themselves and not by their Government. But the Government too was affected. The press might disparage or belaud a statesman, but that statesman now broadcast *urbi et orbi*, and the whole nation could hear, and judge, his words.

The awakened sleeper observed another thing. The cities were straggling into the country as never before, but the nation was becoming alive to the loss. It was as if the perils and discomforts of war had made people more conscious of their heritage of ancient peace. The old distinction between town-dweller and country-dweller was less rigid. New means of transport took the urban population easily to remote places, the interest in wild nature was spreading, men and women, whose eyes had once looked scarcely beyond their own street, were now alive to the riches of their native land. But if Britain awoke to the consciousness of a great possession, this awakening would mean desecration unless the possession were protected. The country-side, so long neglected, was rediscovered and christened " rural England," and there was a vigorous movement to preserve rustic beauty, now badly scarred but not beyond hope, a movement springing not from the few but from the many.

III

After every great effort there is a natural expectation of some quickening and sublimation of the human soul. It may take the form of a religious revival, or a sudden flowering of the creative mind. The war with Spain was followed by the Puritan kindling of the religious consciousness, by Shakespeare and Milton ; the war with Napoleon by the romantic revival in letters and the zealous evangelicalism of the early nineteenth century. But the Great War had no such fruit. The instinct of men to huddle into groups for comfort did indeed produce a few mob-religions, and the dislocation of things and the break-down of old standards brought forth a host of new literary modes. But there was no strong creative impulse to be discerned, or any notable enlargement of spirit. The struggle had taken too heavy a toll of human vitality.

The characteristic note of the first post-War years was a certain peevishness. A thing had only to have won general acceptance in the past to be flouted. A starveling intellectualism discounted whatever to the ordinary mind seemed moving and heroic. A kind of minor history became popular, in which the writers strove to strip the aura from every great character or great drama of the past, like some Greek of the decadence who chipped the nose of an Apollo of Pheidias in order to make the Goths laugh. In fiction the fashion was for the cloacal or the minutely analytic ; in poetry for a breakdown of all shape and a petulant defiance of the orthodox. At the same time an antiquarian spirit was abroad ; obscure ancients were disinterred and deified, and the *pastiche* became a fashionable form. In belief, in morals, and in art there was a craze for dis-integration, which sought to reduce solid things to mere nebulæ of atoms. The prevalent mood was one of bitterness and disillusion, and, since the older standards were rejected, of an extreme arrogance. To be modern was the only proof of quality, and the " post-War mind," brittle and insecure, was regarded as the ultimate flowering of the human spirit. All the familiar clichés of a decadence were in use, and an imperfect education prevented the users from realising how hoary were their darling novelties. This intellectual temper was matched in social life by a kind of joyless gaiety, without manners or grace.

Anxious elders in their haste set down the new youth as trivial in soul and shallow in mind.

The mood did not last. At first the younger generation, more demoralised by the War than those who had fought in it, clamoured only for a safe niche and a " soft option " in life. Ease and security seemed the only ends. But presently youth found its bearings again. In letters there appeared a manlier strain, a return of confidence, humanity and hope. The writers might be extravagant and wildly empirical, but they were cheerfully facing a new world and striving after a new interpretation. If they had not found a gospel they recognised the need of one. To those who had the chance of seeing much of the youth of Britain, the change between the beginning and the end of the post-War decade seemed little short of a miracle. In spite of growing difficulties in making a living, young men carried their heads high. It was as if they realised that they were living in a rough world, and must make certain that there was no hardship in it which they could not face. There was an honest craving for discipline and construction, for they had grown tired of the atomist and the disintegrator. The appeal to many of creeds like communism and fascism was simply the opportunity they gave for sacrifice. The new temper had its perils, but it had also its splendid promise. The idealism, which seemed to have gone to earth after peace, was now again abroad in the world. There was visible, too, one incontrovertible gain from the War. It had done much to break down class barriers and kill a shoddy gentility. The young man of the educated classes to-day is at home, as his father could never have been, in a Hull trawler, or working on the soil with unemployed miners, or lending a hand with the Canadian harvest. He is tougher in fibre, more resourceful, more human.

IV

The older histories were built up on the fortunes of cabinets and parliaments. Politics were " decontrolled," like other things, when the Coalition Cabinet fell in the autumn of 1922, but the Governments which ensued were not the milestones in the national progress which Governments had once been. Mr. Bonar Law succeeded Mr. Lloyd George, and, when ill-health compelled him to resign, he was followed by Mr. Baldwin. The election in the autumn of 1923 brought for the first time a Labour Government into office, a minority Government dependent on Liberal votes. It fell in the next autumn, and for five years the Conservatives were in power with a great majority. In 1929 a Labour Government was again installed, also a minority Government, and in 1931 came the economic crisis and the formation of a National Government under the Labour Prime Minister. But, except the last, these were changes of no profound significance. Any Government, whatever its election programme, had to face the same problems as its predecessor, and very much in the same way. Urgent facts had played havoc with party creeds. At no time in our history, perhaps, has party interest sunk so low as in recent years. This is due in some degree to the fact that our democracy is now plebiscitary, and with universal franchise an election has become a scuffle and a gamble as compared with the old, well-planned contests. But it is largely due to the fact that in a crisis like war or impending bankruptcy the ordinary party business means little. Its use will come again, but that day is not yet.

Few of the men remain who were the foremost public figures before and during the War. The great sailors survive, but of the generals Haig and three of his army commanders are gone. Asquith and Balfour, Curzon and Milner have taken with them some of the high traditions of an earlier Britain, dignity in speech and demeanour, subtlety and precision of thought, a passionate belief in an imperial mission, and a supreme administrative talent. This is not the place to write of those who are left, except to say that the succession is not broken. War left a lamentable gap in our youth, but happily there are brilliant younger figures to bridge that gap. One fact may be noted. The War and the first years of peace did not increase the prestige of Parliament, but the downfall of constitutional government in Europe has revived it. Once again Parliament means much to our people, a thing of their own contriving which they will defend against all attacks, since it is intertwined with their liberties. It is an opportune moment, if statesmen are wise, for that reform in its procedure and in its mode of election which will fit it to meet the stresses of a new age. Plebiscitary democracy, unless it be wisely regulated, may relapse into a meaningless see-saw.

In the disorder of the world every people has felt the need of concentration. This has been done elsewhere by nations surrendering their wills to dictators and camarillas. Britain, with a wiser instinct, has clung to her old institutions, but has modified them to meet new needs. The formation of a National Government in August 1931 was typical of our land, which brought to the task all her constitutional resources. And not least the Throne. On August 21st the King arrived at Balmoral for his Scottish holiday ; next day he returned to London. It was not for him to have any economic policy or any preference as between parties. The common procedure would have been for Mr. Macdonald to resign, and give place to the Conservatives. But, as the trustee of the nation, the King felt that a national emergency should be faced by a national front. His view was accepted by Ministers, and a National Government was formed. That it was also the desire of the people the ensuing election gave instant proof.

EPILOGUE

TO cast the mind back over the last twenty-five years is to survey changes such as no other quarter-century in our record can show. Never before has the nation faced such stupendous " varieties of untried being." But in a season of startling breaches with the past one thing has been unbroken ; one ancient institution has provided the cord on which mutations have been strung—a cord stretching back to our earliest annals. That cord, which has often been thin and sometimes frayed, is now a sevenfold cable. What has become of the solemn nineteenth-century flirtings with republicanism ? The whole nation, the whole Empire, is royalist to-day, not only in constitutional doctrine but in personal affection.

One recent event was proof of this loyalty. In November 1928, at the Armistice Day celebrations, the King caught a chill which developed into a dangerous pleurisy. In December an operation followed, and at Christmastime a shadow hung over the Palace. The Prince of Wales was brought back in haste from Central Africa, a Council of State took over the royal duties, and the people waited anxiously for news, as if the sick man had been their closest kin. The treatment of the malady was a fine example of medical team-work, but the chief hope lay in the patient's resolute courage. Early in the New Year the crisis was passed, and in February the King was able to leave London for the south coast. On April 22nd he issued a message to the Empire :

In looking back on my long illness and recovery, my heart is full of thankfulness of far deeper origin than any mere sense of relief.

I have been brought back from the danger and weariness of the past months by the wonderful skill and devotion of my doctors, surgeons and nurses. And help has come from another source of strength ; as month after month went by I heard of the widespread and loving solicitude with which the Queen and I were surrounded. I was able to picture to myself the crowds of friends waiting and watching at my gates, and to think of the still greater number of those who, in every part of the Empire, were remembering me with prayers and good wishes. The realisation of this has been among the most vivid experiences of my life.

It was an encouragement beyond description to find that my constant and earnest desire had been granted—the desire to gain the confidence and affection of my people. My thoughts have carried me even further than this. I cannot dwell upon the generous sympathy shown to me by unknown friends in many other countries without a new and moving hope. I long to believe it possible that experiences such as mine may soon appear no longer exceptional ; when the national anxieties of all the peoples of the world shall be felt as a common source of human sympathy and a common claim on human friendship.

I am not yet able to bear the strain of a public ceremony, but I look forward on some appointed day to joining with my people at home and overseas in thanking Almighty God, not merely for my own recovery, but for the new evidences of the growing kindliness significant of the true nature of men and nations.

The Thanksgiving Service was held in Westminster Abbey on July 7th, but no ceremony could be more impressive than these simple words of the King. His illness had evoked a passion of loyal concern which was without a parallel. Science may discover some formula for the miracles which may be wrought, even in the physical sphere, by the concentrated will of great masses of men. Our ancestors, more piously and perhaps more wisely, would have attributed his recovery to the prayers of his people.

Majesty and Grace are in the royal office. Monarchy in some form is universal to-day, for it seems to be a necessity in government. Elsewhere it is elective and temporary, as in republics ; or, as in dictatorships, enforced and undefined in term. But a hereditary monarchy is not only more enduring than such types, it has a special quality which they can never win. A king, who reigns not by election or by a sudden popular impulse but by right, has a sanction behind him which no transient dictator or president can claim. His authority is interwoven with the life and thought of his people. If, as in Britain, his ancestry goes back to our dim beginnings, the office embodies the whole history of the nation. Because it is beyond popular caprice, it is, as I have said, the centre of the nation's conscious unity, a link between its past and its future. It becomes a symbol, which needs no artificial sanctity to give it power. With this firm foundation Britain is enabled to be a bold pioneer in new construction, just as the man who would cast his spear far must first find solid footing. It preserves her from the wastefulness of revolution, and from the futile type of revolution which we call reaction.

It has another supreme virtue. The essence of the British monarchy is that the King, while lifted far above the nation, should also be the nation itself in its most characteristic form. There is no place on our Throne for the superman, whether he be conqueror or dreamer ; its occupant must be recognised by his subjects as of like nature with themselves, exalted indeed, but with the same outlook on life, the same traditions and tastes, the same staunch and familiar virtues. " The Englishman," as Goldsmith wrote, " is taught to love the King as his friend " ; and friendship involves a noble equality. In the Platonic utopia the king was the philosopher ; it is more important that he should be the plain man.

The office in itself is a great thing, but it may be made more potent by the personality of him who holds it. It is not for a subject, in Dr. Johnson's famous words, to " bandy civilities with his Sovereign." But the historian must record that the King has added to the duties of the Crown a graciousness which springs from his own character. He has given to ceremonial the bloom of friendliness. He has always possessed a high seriousness, and the note of faith and piety which he has often struck has not been the mere convention of his office. He has walked securely in more difficult constitutional paths than any of his immediate predecessors. He has faced courageously crises which imperilled both his people and his Throne. But, in addition to all this, he has diffused a spirit of simplicity and charity which has profoundly affected the national temper. His quick sympathy and kindliness have warmed the country, and done something to warm a chilly world. When nerve was breaking his steadfastness has restored it, and when strife was fermenting he has spoken the healing word. The power of the Throne lies in what it is : but the authority of the King lies both in what he is, and in what he has done. With the Queen and his family to aid him, he has made Britain not only a nation but a household.

Leadership does not consist only in a strong man

imposing his will upon others. In that sense it has no meaning for a British Sovereign. But in a far profounder sense the King has shown himself a leader, since the true task of leadership is not to put greatness into humanity, but to elicit it, since the greatness is already there. That truth is the basis of all religion, it is the only justification for democracy, it is the chart and compass of our mortal life. The King has led his people, for he has evoked what is best in them.

INDEX

279

INDEX

INDEX

INDEX

INDEX

INDEX

INDEX

The Coronation Group, 1911

The Coronation Procession outside Westminster Abbey, 1911

Driving to the Coronation Durbar, 1912

At the Coronation Durbar

Photo : Daily Mirror

His Majesty the King in 1912

Photo : W. & D. Downey

Four Generations

The Visit to Dublin, 1911

At the University College of South Wales, 1912

The King and Queen at the Opening of Parliament

The Visit to a Yorkshire Coalmine, 1912

The Opening of the Hull Joint Dock, 1914

Photo : W. & D. Downey

The Royal Family

With General Foch at the British Army Manœuvres, 1912

Driving to St. James's Palace with President Poincaré, 1913

Leaving the Hertford British Hospital during the Paris visit, 1914

Photo : S. Cribb, Southsea

The Destroyers passing the King in the Review of July, 1914

Photo : S. Cribb, Southsea

The Coronation Review of the Fleet, 1911

The Royal Visit to Henley in 1912

Leaving Ascot in 1913

Photo : Topical Press

Guests arriving at the Windsor Garden Party, 1912

Photo : Topical Press

Inspecting the *New Zealand* at Portsmouth, 1913

The Investiture of the Prince of Wales at Carnarvon, 1911

The Opening of Parliament, 1912

Lord Kitchener leaving the War Office

Photo : Sport & General

Outside Buckingham Palace, August, 1914

Photo : Sport & General

A scene outside the Foreign Office, August, 1914

A war-time portrait of Admiral Sir John Jellicoe

Viscount Haldane

Mr. Bonar Law

Viscount Grey
of Fallodon

Viscount Milner

Mr. Asquith

Mr. Balfour

Photo : Sport & General

Inspecting R.A.F. cadets

Photo : I.N.A.

Inspecting front line troops in France

The King with Marshal Foch, Field-Marshal Sir Douglas Haig, General Pétain and General Sir Henry Rawlinson

Photo : L.N.A.

Visiting New Zealand troops in France

Photo : L.N.A.

A tour of the trenches

Mr. Lloyd George speaking in 1916

Photo : Imperial War Museum

A scene on the Western Front

Photo : Imperial War Museum

Another battle scene

Photo : Sport & General

An open-air investiture of V.C.s outside Buckingham Palace

At the Canadian Commemoration Service at Westminster Abbey in 1917

Visiting allotments, 1918

Inspecting men from a British Monitor at a French Port

A Y.W.C.A. hut for munition workers

Photo : Sport & General

Cheering nurses and wounded soldiers outside Buckingham Palace,
November 11, 1918

Photo : Sport & General

Cheering the Royal Family during the peace celebrations

Photo : L.N.A.

Proclamation of peace at the Royal Exchange, 1919

Photo : Sport & General

Armistice Day sixteen years later

Photo : Central Press

The Victory March in 1919

Photo : Sport & General

Driving with President Wilson

Photo : Sport & General

Taking the salute at the Peace Procession with Marshal Foch, the Prince of Wales,
the Queen, Queen Alexandra and General Pershing

His Majesty the King.   1923

Photo : Topical Press

Visiting the Wembley Exhibition, 1925

Photo : L.N.A.

At a Children's Hospital in Birmingham

Presenting New Colours to the Royal Horse Guards, 1927

A Royal Garden Party at Buckingham Palace

Leaving St. Paul's after the Thanksgiving Service for the restoration of the Cathedral

Photo : J. Russell & Sons

The Queen in the grounds of Sandringham

The Prince of Wales.   From a drawing by W. Hatherell, R.I.

Photo : Sport & General

The Prince of Wales taking leave of the Royal Family on his departure for India
in 1921

Photo : Daily Mirror

The Empire Thanksgiving Service at Wembley

Photo : L.N.A.

On board the *Britannia* at Cowes

Photo : Sport & General

At the Braemar Gathering

Mr. Ramsay MacDonald.   The first Labour Prime Minister

A food convoy during the General Strike, 1926

The milk distributing centre in Hyde Park during the General Strike

In the State Coach for the opening of Parliament

Mr. Stanley Baldwin at the General Election of 1931